Natalie King

ESSENTIALS

OCR Gateway

GCSE Biology B
Revision Guide

Contents

Contents

Fundamental Scientific Processes

Scientists carry out **experiments** and collect **evidence** in order to explain how and why things happen. Scientific knowledge and understanding can lead to the **development of new technologies** which have a huge impact on **society** and the **environment**.

Scientific evidence is often based on data that has been collected through **observations** and **measurements**. To allow scientists to reach conclusions, evidence must be **repeatable**, **reproducible** and **valid**.

Models

Models are used to explain scientific ideas and the universe around us. Models can be used to describe:
- a complex idea like how heat moves through a metal
- a system like the Earth's structure.

Models make a system or idea easier to understand by only including the most important parts. They can be used to explain real world observations or to make predictions. But, because models don't contain all the variables, they do sometimes make incorrect predictions.

Models and scientific ideas may change as new observations are made and new data are collected. Data and observations may be collected from a series of experiments. For example, the accepted model of the structure of the atom has been modified as new technology and further experiments have produced new evidence.

Hypotheses

Scientific explanations are called hypotheses. Hypotheses are used to explain observations. A hypothesis can be tested by planning experiments and collecting data and evidence. For example, if you pull a metal wire you may observe that it stretches. This can be explained by the scientific idea that the atoms in the metal are in layers and can slide over each other. A hypothesis can be modified as new data is collected, and may even be disproved.

Data

Data can be displayed in **tables**, **pie charts** or **line graphs**. In your exam you may be asked to:
- choose the most appropriate method for displaying data
- identify trends
- use the data mathematically, including using statistical methods, calculating the **mean** and calculating gradients on graphs.

Pie Chart

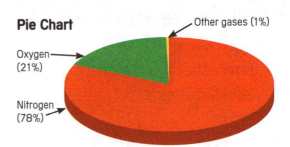

Other gases (1%)
Oxygen (21%)
Nitrogen (78%)

Line Graph

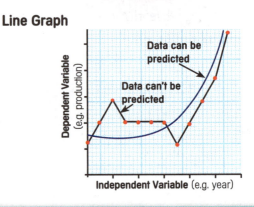

Data can be predicted

Data can't be predicted

Dependent Variable (e.g. production)

Independent Variable (e.g. year)

Table

Pressure (Atmospheres)	Yield (%) Temperature (°C)			
	250	350	450	550
200	73	50	28	13
400	77	65	45	26

Data (Cont.)

Sometimes the same data can lead to different conclusions. For example, data shows that the world's average temperatures have been rising significantly over the last 200 years. Some scientists think this is due to increased combustion of fossil fuels, whilst other scientists think it's a natural change seen before in Earth's history.

Scientific and Technological Development

Every scientific or technological development could have effects that we do not know about. This can give rise to **issues**. An issue is an important question that is in dispute and needs to be settled. Issues could be:

- **Social** – they impact on the human population of a community, city, country, or the world.
- **Environmental** – they impact on the planet, its natural ecosystems and resources.
- **Economic** – money and related factors like employment and the distribution of resources.
- **Cultural** – what is morally right and wrong; a value judgement must be made.

Peer review is a process of self-regulation involving experts in a particular field who **critically examine** the work undertaken. Peer review methods are designed to maintain standards and provide **credibility** for the work that has been carried out. The methods used vary depending on the type of work and also on the overall purpose behind the review process.

Evaluating Information

Conclusions can then be made based on the scientific evidence that has been collected and should try to explain the results and observations.

Evaluations look at the whole investigation. It is important to be able to evaluate information relating to social-scientific issues. When evaluating information:

- make a list of **pluses** (pros)
- make a list of **minuses** (cons)
- consider how each point might **impact on society**.

You also need to consider whether the source of information is reliable and credible and consider opinions, bias and weight of evidence.

Opinions are personal viewpoints. Opinions backed up by valid and reliable evidence carry far more weight than those based on non-scientific ideas. Opinions of experts can also carry more weight than opinions of non-experts. Information is **biased** if it favours one particular viewpoint without providing a balanced account. Biased information might include incomplete evidence or try to influence how you interpret the evidence.

B1 Fitness and Health

The Circulatory System

Your **circulatory system** carries oxygen and glucose in your blood to all your body's cells so that energy can be released through **aerobic respiration**.

Your **heart** pumps blood around your body:

- Your heart **relaxes** to fill with blood.
- Your heart **contracts** to squeeze the blood out into the **arteries**.

When the heart contracts, the blood is put under pressure and is sent into the arteries. This ensures that the blood reaches all parts of the body supplying cells with glucose and oxygen for respiration. This surge of blood is the **heart beat** or **pulse**. Blood in the arteries is always under pressure.

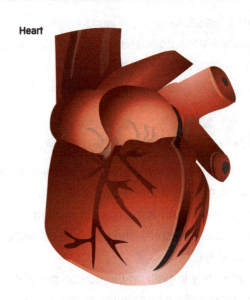

Heart

Blood Pressure

Blood pressure is a measure of the force of blood per unit area as it flows through the arteries. It's measured in **mm Hg (millimetres of mercury)**.

Blood pressure is represented by two measurements, e.g. 120/80 mm Hg:

- **Systolic** blood pressure (the first number) is the pressure in your arteries when your heart contracts, i.e. when blood pressure is at its highest.
- **Diastolic** blood pressure (the second number) is the pressure in your arteries when your heart relaxes.

Normal blood pressure is about 120/80 mm Hg. But, it can be affected by age and lifestyle.

You can reduce high blood pressure and maintain normal blood pressure by doing regular aerobic exercise to strengthen your heart. A healthy diet can also help by keeping weight steady.

Factors that can lead to high blood pressure include:

- Excess weight – the circulatory system has to work harder to pump blood around the body of a person who is overweight.
- High stress levels.
- Excess alcohol.

- A diet which is high in saturated fat, sugar and / or salt. Too much salt can raise blood pressure, whilst too much **saturated fat** can lead to a build-up of **cholesterol** in the arteries forming plaques. The amount of cholesterol in arteries can be linked to the amount of saturated fat eaten. This plaque bulges into the lumen, restricting or blocking blood flow through the arteries, increasing the risk of heart attack.
- Smoking – the carbon monoxide produced reduces the oxygen-carrying capacity of the blood so the heart rate and pressure increases in order to compensate. Plus, nicotine increases the heart rate.

> **HT** Carbon monoxide takes the place of oxygen in the haemoglobin so the oxygen-carrying capacity of the blood is greatly reduced.

Key Words   **Aerobic respiration • Artery • Blood pressure • Cholesterol**

HT Blood Pressure (Cont.)

In the long-term, **high blood pressure** is dangerous because the blood vessels can weaken and eventually burst. If a blood vessel bursts in the brain it may lead to brain damage or a stroke. In the kidneys it may lead to kidney damage.

Low blood pressure means the blood doesn't circulate efficiently, so some parts of the body are deprived of **glucose** and oxygen. This can lead to dizziness, fainting, and cold hands and feet. Pressure may drop in the kidneys, leading to kidney failure.

Causes of Heart Disease

Many factors increase the risk of **heart disease**:

- High blood pressure.
- Smoking – carbon monoxide combines with red blood cells, preventing them from carrying as much oxygen.
- Too much salt.
- High-fat diets.

HT High-fat diets and high cholesterol can block arteries and cause heart attacks. Heart attacks are more likely with narrowed coronary arteries and **thrombosis**.

Health and Fitness

Being **healthy** means being free from infection (i.e. no coughs, colds or diseases).

Being **fit** relates to how much physical activity you're capable of doing and how quickly your body recovers afterwards.

Different types of exercise develop different aspects of fitness, all of which are measurable. For example, strength, stamina, flexibility, agility and speed can all be measured.

Cardiovascular efficiency – how well your heart copes with aerobic exercise and how quickly it recovers afterwards – is often used as a measure of general fitness.

A fit person's heart will return to its normal resting rate much quicker than a less fit person's heart. During exercise, a fitter person will have a lower heart rate than a less fit person.

HT There are many ways to measure fitness. It is best to use a combination of tests, rather than just one, when making decisions on how fit someone is.

A Balanced Diet

Food supplies living organisms with **energy** and **nutrients**. A balanced diet must contain:

- **carbohydrates** and **fats** to provide energy
- **protein** for growth and repair of tissues (and energy, if carbohydrates are in short supply).

Carbohydrates are made of simple sugars such as glucose. **Fats** are made up of fatty acids and glycerol. **Proteins** are made up of **amino acids**.

HT Carbohydrates are stored in the liver as glycogen or can be converted to fats. Fats are stored under the skin and around organs as adipose tissue. Proteins are not stored.

Although they don't provide energy, you also need other substances in your diet to keep your body **healthy**, including:

- **minerals**, e.g. iron to make haemoglobin in red blood cells
- **vitamins**, e.g. vitamin C to prevent scurvy

- **fibre** to prevent constipation and to maintain healthy bowels.
- **water** to prevent dehydration, and to help remove waste.

You might alter your diet as a result of:

- **beliefs** about animal welfare, e.g. vegetarians, vegans
- **religious beliefs**, e.g. the Muslim and Jewish faiths prohibit the eating of pig meat
- **medical issues**, and food allergies, e.g. some people are allergic to peanuts
- **age** – older people need less food (fewer calories); younger people need more calories (as they are more active) and more protein
- **sex** – males need more calories due to being larger and having more muscle
- **activity** – someone with a physical job, e.g. a builder, will need more calories than an office worker
- **personal choice.**

How Much Energy is Needed?

The amount of **energy** you need depends on your age, sex and activity levels.

To maintain a healthy **body mass**, you must **balance** the amount of energy you consume with the amount of energy you use up through daily activity.

You can calculate your **Body Mass Index (BMI)** using this formula:

$$BMI = \frac{Mass\ (kg)}{Height\ (m)^2}$$

Then you can find your BMI in the chart to see what it means.

BMI	What it Means
<18.5	Underweight (too light for your height)
18.5–24.9	Ideal weight (correct weight for your height)
25-29.9	Overweight (too heavy for your height)
>30	Obese (much too heavy; health risks)

If you consume more food than you need, you will become very overweight or obese.

Obesity is a major health problem in the developed world. It can lead to arthritis (swollen and painful joints), heart disease, type II **diabetes** and breast cancer.

Protein

Protein molecules are long chains of **amino acids**.

 • **Essential** amino acids must be taken in by eating food (your body can't make them).

• **Non-essential** amino acids can be made in your body.

Protein supplies the nutrients that enable you to grow. This is why it's important for teenagers to have a high-protein diet.

HT Proteins from animal origin are called **first class proteins**. Meat and fish are first class proteins because they contain all the essential amino acids (which cannot be made by the body). Plant proteins are called second class proteins.

In some parts of the world (i.e. developing countries), food is in very short supply, so people don't get enough protein in their diet.

In children, protein **deficiency** results in a disease called **kwashiorkor**. This disease is common in developing countries due to overpopulation and limited investment in agriculture.

You can calculate your **estimated average daily requirement** for protein (**EAR**) using this formula:

$$\text{EAR} = 0.6 \times \text{Body mass (kg)}$$

Protein is only used as an energy source when carbohydrates or fats are not available.

HT EAR is an estimated daily figure for an average person of a certain body mass. It can vary depending on age, pregnancy and lactation (i.e. whether a woman is producing milk).

Poor Diets and Eating Disorders

Low self-esteem, poor self-image and a desire for perfection can all lead to a poor diet.

Poor diets can be very damaging to the body. The body doesn't get the balance of energy and nutrients needed to function correctly. The reproduction system may be affected as well as damage to the bones.

Eating disorders such as anorexia nervosa or bulimia nervosa may result.

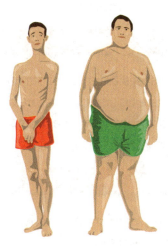

Quick Test

1 What factors affect blood pressure?
2 How can you calculate your BMI?
3 What diseases are linked to obesity?
4 Why is kwashiorkor mainly found in developing countries?

B1 Staying Healthy

Non-Infectious Diseases

Non-infectious diseases can't be caught from another person. There are many causes:

- **Poor diet**, e.g. a lack of vitamin C causes scurvy, and a lack of iron causes anaemia.
- **Organ malfunction**, e.g. the pancreas stops producing insulin (which causes diabetes).

- **Genetic inheritance**, e.g. people inherit the genes for a particular disease from their parent, e.g. red–green colour blindness.
- **Cells mutate** and become **cancerous**.

These diseases are different to infectious diseases in that they can't be 'caught' or passed on. No **pathogens** are involved.

Cancer

Cancer is a **non-infectious** disease where cells grow out of control and form tumours.

Making healthy lifestyle choices is one way to reduce the likelihood of getting cancer, for example:

- Don't smoke – chemicals in cigarettes cause lung cancer and other cancers like throat cancer.
- Don't drink excess alcohol – alcohol is linked to cancer of the liver, gut and mouth.
- Avoid getting sunburn – skin cells damaged by the sun can become cancerous.
- Eat a healthy diet – a high-fibre diet can reduce the risk of bowel cancer.

HT Cancerous cells divide in an abnormal and uncontrolled way, forming lumps of cells called **tumours**.

A tumour that grows in one place is described as **benign**. But, if cells break off and secondary tumours start to grow in other parts of the body, the tumour is described as **malignant**.

A person's chance of **survival** depends on the type of cancer they have. The chance of survival is greater if the cancer is diagnosed early, the patient is young and the tumour is benign.

Infectious Diseases

Infectious diseases are spread from one person to another. They are diseases you can catch. They are caused by **pathogens**, which are **microorganisms** that attack and invade the body.

Examples include **fungi**, **viruses**, **bacteria** and **protozoa**. For example, athlete's foot is caused by a fungus, flu is caused by a virus, cholera is caused by a bacterium and malaria is caused by a protozoan.

Malaria

Some diseases, for example, **malaria**, are spread by organisms called **vectors**:

1. A mosquito (the **vector**) sucks blood from a human (the **host** where the vectors live).
2. If there are malaria **parasites** (organisms that live off other organisms) in the blood, they mate and move from the mosquito's gut to its salivary glands.
3. The mosquito bites another person and passes the malaria parasites into their bloodstream.
4. The malaria parasites move to the liver, where they mature and reproduce.
5. The new generation of malaria parasites migrates to the blood and replicates in red blood cells, bursting them open. This damage leads to characteristic malaria fever and can sometimes result in death.

Key Words   **Pathogen • Benign • Malignant • Fungi • Virus • Bacteria • Protozoa**

(HT) Malaria (Cont.)

Knowledge of the life cycle of a disease and the way in which vectors spread the disease can help in controlling it. For example, malaria can be prevented by controlling the vector (the mosquito) by:
- sleeping under mosquito nets
- using insect repellents
- killing mosquitoes with insecticide.

By taking these precautions, the spread of the disease is greatly reduced.

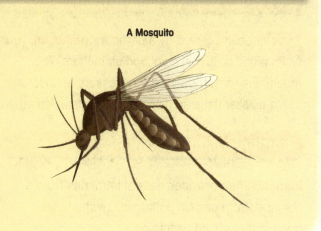

A Mosquito

Defences Against Pathogens

The body has a number of **defences** to stop pathogens getting in:
- The **skin** acts as a barrier against microorganisms.
- The **blood clots** in wounds to prevent microorganisms from entering the bloodstream.

- The **respiratory system** is lined with cells that produce a sticky, liquid mucus that forms a mucus membrane to trap microorganisms.
- The **stomach** produces **hydrochloric acid** which kills microorganisms in the food we eat.

Dealing with Pathogens Inside the Body

If **pathogens** enter the body, **white blood cells** start fighting the invasion. The symptoms of a disease are caused by **pathogens** damaging cells and **producing toxins** (poisons) before the white blood cells can destroy them.

There are two types of white blood cell, which deal with pathogens in two ways:
- By engulfing and digesting pathogens they find in the bloodstream.
- By making **antibodies** to attack pathogens. They recognise markers (**antigens**) on the surface of the pathogen and produce antibodies which lock onto the markers (antigens), killing the pathogens.

(HT) Every pathogen has **unique antigens** (markers). White blood cells make **antibodies** specifically for a particular antigen, e.g. antibodies made to fight tetanus have no effect on whooping cough or cholera.

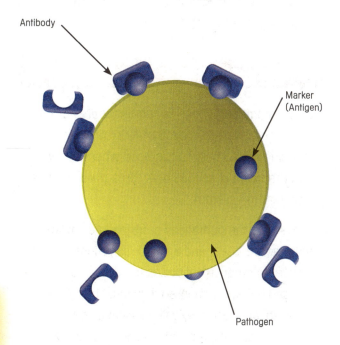

A White Blood Cell Making Antibodies

Antibody

Marker (Antigen)

Pathogen

B1 Staying Healthy

Natural (Active) Immunity

If you've been infected by a particular **pathogen**, your white blood cells make **antibodies** to them. This means they can produce the necessary antibodies much quicker if the same pathogen is detected again.

This provides future **protection** against the disease and is called **natural** or **active immunity**.

The antibodies stay in the blood for years to fight future infections.

Immunisation/Vaccination

Immunisation provides natural immunity from a disease (from certain pathogens), without you being infected and becoming ill.

HT Immunisation (vaccination) works as follows:

1. A person is **injected** with a weakened or dead strain of the pathogen, which is incapable of multiplying. It's harmless.

2. Even though the pathogens are harmless, the antigens (markers) **trigger** the production of specific **antibodies** by the white blood cells.

3. Long after the pathogen has been dealt with, the white blood cells remain **in the blood** (memory cells are produced). This means more antibodies can be produced very quickly if the same pathogen is detected again.

Benefits of immunisation:

- It **protects** against diseases which could kill or cause disability, e.g. polio, measles.
- If everybody is vaccinated, the disease can't spread and eventually **dies out**. (This is what happened to smallpox.)

Risks of immunisation:

- An individual could have a **bad reaction** to the vaccine.
- No vaccination is 100% safe, but the benefits outweigh the risks.

Passive Immunity

Passive immunity occurs when **antibodies** are put into an individual's body, rather than the body producing them itself. This is used when a very quick response is needed or when a person has a weak immune system.

For example, the **pathogens** or **toxins** in a snake's venom act very fast, and a person's immune system is unable to produce antibodies to destroy the pathogen quickly enough, so they must be injected with antibodies. But, they will not have long-term protection against the pathogen because their white blood cells didn't produce the antibodies themselves. After a while, they will have no antibodies for that antigen left in their blood.

Treating Diseases with Drugs

Diseases caused by bacteria or fungi (not viruses) can be treated using **antibiotics**. These chemicals kill bacteria and fungi.

Antiviral drugs are used to treat diseases caused by viruses only.

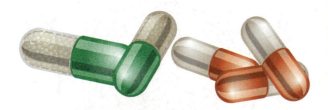

HT Antibiotics are very effective at killing bacteria. But, if doctors over-prescribe antibiotics, all the bacteria in a population are killed off except the **resistant** ones, which then spread. So, the antibiotic then becomes useless.

MRSA is a bacteria which has become resistant to most antibiotics, making it a dangerous microorganism that the media has dubbed a '**superbug**'.

Careful use of antibiotics is needed to prevent more resistant bacterial infections occurring.

Testing New Drugs

New drugs have to be tested to make sure that they are effective and safe before they can be made available to the public.

A drug can be tested using:
- **computer models** to predict how it will affect cells, based on known information about how the body works and the effects of similar drugs
- **animals** to see how it affects living organisms (many people object on the grounds of animal cruelty)
- **human tissue** (grown in a laboratory) to see how it affects human cells. (Some people object to human tissue being grown in this way because they believe it's unnatural and wrong.)

Finally, the drug must be tested on **healthy volunteers**, and on **volunteers** who have the **disease**. Some are given the new drug and some are given a **placebo** (an inactive pill). The effects of the drug can then be compared to the effects of taking the placebo.

Although scientists conduct lots of tests beforehand to determine how the drugs will affect humans, drug trials like these can never be completely safe.

HT In a **blind trial**, the volunteers don't know whether they have been given the new drug or the placebo. This eliminates any psychological factors and helps to provide a fair comparison.

In a **double blind trial**, neither the volunteers nor the doctors know which pill has been given. This eliminates all bias from the test, because the doctors can't influence the volunteers' responses in any way.

Quick Test

1. Give three examples of pathogens.
2. **HT** Briefly describe immunisation (vaccination).
3. **HT** How can you prevent the spread of malaria?

B1 The Nervous System

The Nervous System

Your **nervous system** allows you to **react** to your surroundings and **coordinate** your behaviour. It comprises the **central nervous system** (CNS) and the **peripheral nervous system** (PNS), which includes receptors and neurones.

Animals detect changes in their environment (**stimuli**) using **receptors**, specialised nerve endings that generate nerve impulses. You have:

- light receptors in your eyes
- sound receptors and balance receptors in your ears
- taste receptors on your tongue
- smell receptors in your nose
- touch, pressure, pain and temperature receptors in your skin.

The Main Components of the Nervous System

Brain

Spinal cord

The neurones that make up the peripheral nervous system

CNS (brain and spinal cord)

Neurones

Neurones (nerve cells) are specially adapted cells that can carry a **nerve impulse**. Nerve impulses are electrical messages/signals and are carried along the **axon** (the long, thin part of the cell).

There are three types of neurone:

- **Sensory neurones** carry nerve impulses from the receptors to your brain.
- **Relay neurones** make connections between neurones inside your brain and your spinal cord.
- **Motor neurones** carry nerve impulses from your brain to your muscles and glands.

A Motor Neurone

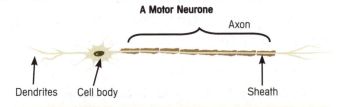

Axon

Dendrites   Cell body   Sheath

HT Neurones are adapted to their job. They have:

- an **elongated** (long) **shape** (axon) to make connections from one part of the body to another
- an **insulating sheath** to speed up the nerve impulse
- **dendrites** (branched endings) to allow a single neurone to act on many muscle fibres.

HT Synapses

1. An electrical impulse travels down a neurone until it reaches a synapse (a small gap between neurones).
2. A transmitter substance diffuses across the synapse (gap).
3. The transmitter binds with receptor molecules on the next neurone, causing an electrical impulse to be initiated in that neurone. The message goes:

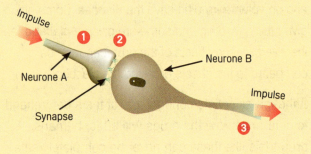

Impulse

1   2

Neurone B

Neurone A

Synapse

Impulse

3

Neurone A → **Synapse** → **Neurone B**
(Electrical message)   (Chemical message)   (Electrical message)

Receptor • Neurone • Synapse

Voluntary Actions and Reflex Actions

Voluntary actions are under the **conscious** control of your brain, i.e. **you decide** how to react to a stimulus. For example, tasting something bitter (stimulus) and spitting it out (response).

Reflex actions (or involuntary responses) **bypass** your brain to give fast, **automatic** responses to a stimulus, to help protect your body from harm, e.g:

- pupil reflex automatically controls light entering your eye (to prevent damage to your retina)
- knee jerk reaction
- automatically withdrawing your hand from a hot plate to prevent you from getting burned.

The pathway that the message takes is called the **reflex arc**.

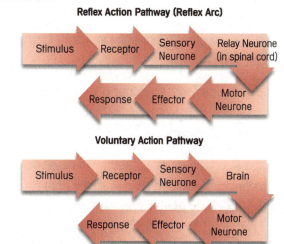

Reflex Action Pathway (Reflex Arc)

Stimulus → Receptor → Sensory Neurone → Relay Neurone (in spinal cord) → Motor Neurone → Effector → Response

Voluntary Action Pathway

Stimulus → Receptor → Sensory Neurone → Brain → Motor Neurone → Effector → Response

The Eye

Your **iris** (the coloured part of the eye) controls the amount of light that enters your eye. The rays of **light** are **refracted** by your **cornea**, and the **lens** focuses light onto the **retina** so the rays **converge** (come together) at a single point and produce a clear **image** on your retina. The light-sensitive receptor cells on your retina then cause nerve impulses to pass along sensory neurones in the **optic nerve** to your brain. The retina contains the light-sensitive receptors. Some are sensitive to colour.

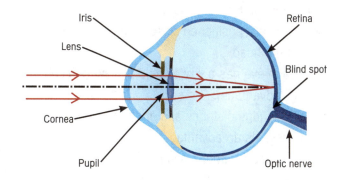

Labels: Iris, Lens, Cornea, Pupil, Retina, Blind spot, Optic nerve

HT The **lens** is a clear, flexible bag of fluid surrounded by circular **ciliary** muscles that change the shape of the lens (accommodation). **Suspensory** ligaments attach the lens to the ciliary muscles.

When receiving light rays from a near object:

- the ciliary muscles contract
- the suspensory ligaments relax
- the lens is short and fat to refract light a lot.

When receiving light rays from a distant object:

- the ciliary muscles relax
- the suspensory ligaments contract
- the lens is long and thin because the light only needs to be refracted a little.

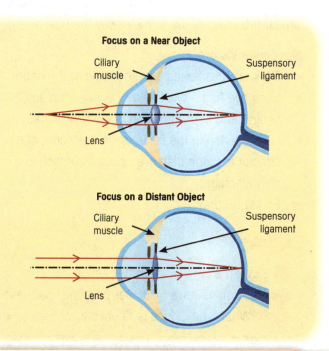

Focus on a Near Object

Labels: Ciliary muscle, Suspensory ligament, Lens

Focus on a Distant Object

Labels: Ciliary muscle, Suspensory ligament, Lens

Eye Defects

Common eye defects are:

- long sight
- short sight
- red–green colour blindness (an inherited condition).

In people with red–green colour blindness, some of the specialised cells in the retina that detect red and green light are missing.

Long and short sight are caused by the eyeball or the lens being the wrong **shape**, so the light rays can't be accurately **focused** on the retina.

HT Long and short sight can be corrected by contact lenses, glasses, or laser surgery. Long sight can be corrected by wearing a convex lens and short sight can be corrected by wearing a concave lens.

Corrective laser eye surgery works by cutting a flap in the cornea, folding it back and using a laser to reshape the cornea. With the shape of the cornea corrected, clear vision is returned and the light rays are now accurately focused on the retina.

Types of Vision

Binocular vision:

- Eyes are positioned close together on the front of the head.
- Each eye has a limited field of view (which is a disadvantage).
- Can judge distance and speed accurately (which is an advantage).
- Found on humans and predators.

The brain uses binocular vision to judge distances by comparing the images from each eye. The more similar the images, the further away the object.

Monocular vision:

- Eyes are positioned on either side of the head.
- Each eye has a wide field of view – can see behind and in front (which is an advantage).
- Little overlap in the fields of view which makes it difficult to judge distance or speed (which is a disadvantage).
- Found on prey.

Binocular Vision

Monocular Vision

Quick Test

1. Give an example of a reflex action.
2. Do humans have binocular or monocular vision?
3. HT What type of lens is needed to correct long sight?

Drugs

Drugs are **chemicals** that affect your mind or body. All **beneficial** drugs, i.e. medicines, are **legal**. But some medicines can have bad side effects if not used correctly, which is why they're only available on prescription. Most **harmful** drugs are **illegal**.

Drugs are **categorised** according to the effects they produce when taken:

- **Stimulants** (e.g. caffeine, nicotine, ecstasy) increase brain activity which leads to a feeling of alertness and heightened perception.
- **Depressants** (e.g. alcohol, solvents, tranquillisers like temazepam) decrease brain activity which makes you feel tired, and slows down your reactions. It can lead to a feeling of lethargy and forgetfulness.
- **Painkillers** or anaesthetics (e.g. aspirin, Paracetamol, heroin) reduce pain by blocking nerve impulses.
- **Performance-enhancing drugs** (e.g. anabolic steroids) increase muscle development, which is why they're sometimes abused by sports people.
- **Hallucinogens** (e.g. LSD) distort what is seen and heard.

HT Stimulants and depressants act on the synapses of the nervous system. Stimulants cause more neuro-transmitters to cross the synapse. This speeds up the nervous impulses.

Depressants bind with receptor molecules in the membrane of the next neurone, blocking the transmission of the impulse. This slows everything down.

In the UK, illegal drugs are classified into three main categories under the Misuse of Drugs Act:

- **Class A** drugs (e.g. heroin, cocaine) are the most dangerous and carry heavy prison sentences and fines for possession.
- **Class B** drugs (including amphetamines, e.g. speed and barbiturates) have lower penalties.
- **Class C** drugs (e.g. tranquilisers and anabolic steroids) are less dangerous and have the lowest penalties.

Addiction and Rehabilitation

Drug **addiction** is a state of psychological or physical need for a drug. As an addict's body becomes more used to the drug, it develops a **tolerance** to it, i.e. the addict needs higher doses of the drug to get the same effects.

When a drug addict stops taking a drug they can suffer from **withdrawal** symptoms, including:

- **psychological** problems, e.g. cravings
- **physical** problems, e.g. sweating, shaking, nausea.

Rehabilitation is the process by which an addict learns to live without the drug. This takes a long time because their body and mind both have to adapt.

B1 Drugs and You

Alcohol

Drinking **excess alcohol** can lead to unconsciousness and even coma or death.

Short-term effects of drinking alcohol include:
- lack of balance and muscle control
- blurred vision and slurred speech
- poor judgement and drowsiness
- vasodilation – the blood vessels widen, increasing blood flow to skin and heat loss.

Long-term effects of drinking alcohol include:
- liver damage, due to the liver working very hard to remove the **toxic** alcohol from the body
- brain damage due to dehydration.

HT The liver contains enzymes which break down alcohol. But, the products of breakdown are toxic and cause liver damage.

Cirrhosis of the liver (i.e. damage to the liver as a result of liver disease) is a common disease amongst heavy drinkers.

The legal blood alcohol content limit for driving is 80 milligrams of alcohol per 100 millilitres of blood. This limit has been set because alcohol slows reaction times, increasing the chance of accidents. The limit is even less for aeroplane pilots.

Tobacco

Smoking can lead to several diseases, including **cancer** of the mouth, throat, oesophagus and lungs, heart disease, **emphysema** and bronchitis. Smoking damages the **cilia** (ciliated epithelial cells), which line the airways (**trachea**, **bronchi** and **bronchioles**). This prevents the cilia from being able to remove the mucus, tar and dirt from the lungs, which leads to a 'smoker's cough' as the body tries to cough up mucus. Excess coughing can damage the alveoli and cause emphysema.

This smoking machine experiment (alongside) shows that cigarettes contain **tar**. Cigarettes also contain **nicotine,** which is very addictive, and produce **carbon monoxide** and particulates when they are burned. The carbon monoxide produced by a burning cigarette is dangerous because the blood picks it up instead of picking up oxygen. This means the blood is carrying much less oxygen. This leaves smokers feeling breathless and can lead to heart disease.

Tar contains chemicals that are **irritants** and **carcinogens** (cancer-causing chemicals). **Particulates** in cigarette smoke accumulate in living tissue, e.g. lung tissue which can cause cancer.

It's currently illegal to smoke in enclosed public places in the UK. Do you agree with this?

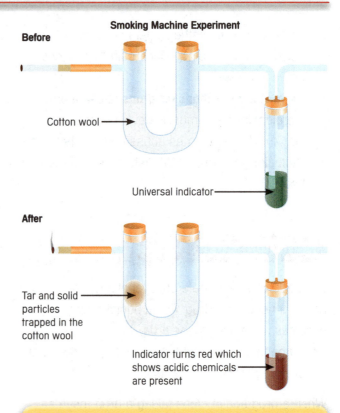

Smoking Machine Experiment

Before

Cotton wool

Universal indicator

After

Tar and solid particles trapped in the cotton wool

Indicator turns red which shows acidic chemicals are present

Quick Test

1. List two short-term effects of drinking alcohol.
2. What colour does the indicator change to on the smoking machine and why?
3. What part of cigarette smoke is carcinogenic?

Alcohol • Emphysema • Carcinogens

Homeostasis

Your body has automatic control systems to maintain a constant internal environment to ensure that cells can function efficiently. This is called **homeostasis**. It is the maintenance of a constant internal environment.

Your body **balances** inputs and outputs to keep the internal environment steady, e.g. steady temperature, steady water levels and steady carbon dioxide levels in the blood.

Temperature Control

Enzymes in your body work best at **37°C**, so it's essential that your body remains very close to this temperature. Heat produced through respiration is used to maintain your body temperature.

If body temperature becomes too **high**, blood vessels widen and the blood flows closer to the skin so heat can be transferred to the environment. This is also done by sweating – the evaporation of sweat requires heat energy to be removed from the skin.

Getting too hot can be very dangerous. If too much water is lost through sweating, the body becomes **dehydrated**. This can lead to **heat stroke** and even **death**.

If the body temperature falls too **low**, blood vessels constrict and the blood flow near the skin is reduced, sweating stops and muscles start making tiny contractions, commonly known as shivers. These contractions need energy from respiration, and heat is released as a by-product.

Getting too cold can be fatal. **Hypothermia** is when the body temperature drops below 35°C. This causes **unconsciousness** and sometimes **death**. Putting on more clothing and doing exercise can help to raise body temperature.

Body temperature readings can be taken from the mouth, ear, skin surface, finger or anus. Although an anal temperature reading is the most accurate, it's normally only used in hospitals. Digital recording probes and thermal imaging are also used in hospitals. At home, heat-sensitive strips that are placed on the forehead are an alternative to clinical **thermometers**, which go under the tongue.

HT Blood temperature is **monitored** by the **brain**, which switches various temperature control mechanisms on and off. **Vasodilation** and **vasoconstriction** are the widening and narrowing (respectively) of the blood vessels close to the skin's surface in order to increase or reduce heat loss by radiation.

Negative feedback involves the automatic reversal of a change in condition. It occurs frequently in homeostasis. For example, if the temperature falls too low, the brain switches on mechanisms to raise it. If the temperature then becomes too high, the brain switches on mechanisms to lower it.

Blood temperature is monitored by the brain using the nervous system and the hormonal system. Temperature control systems work to keep a constant temperature.

Vasodilation – When the Body is too Warm

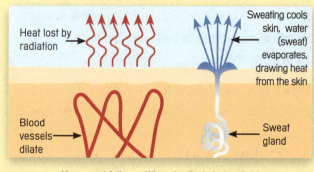

Vasoconstriction – When the Body is too Cold

B1 Staying in Balance

Hormones

Hormones are chemical messages released by **glands** directly into the bloodstream. They travel around the body to their target organs.

Hormones travel much **slower** (at the speed of blood) than a nervous impulse, which is an electrical message relayed directly to the target organs.

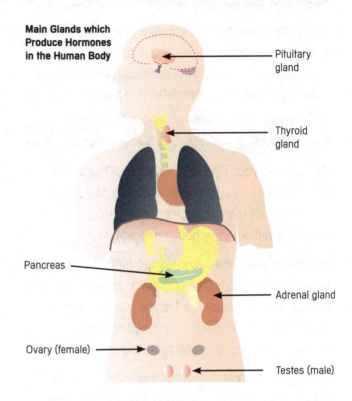

Main Glands which Produce Hormones in the Human Body

- Pituitary gland
- Thyroid gland
- Pancreas
- Adrenal gland
- Ovary (female)
- Testes (male)

Diabetes

The hormone **insulin** is released by the pancreas to control blood sugar levels. Insulin travels in the blood.

Type I diabetes is caused by the pancreas failing to produce **insulin**. This can lead to blood sugar levels rising fatally high and resulting in a **coma** or death. So blood sugar has to be controlled by injecting insulin into the blood.

Type II diabetes affects the cells that respond to insulin. They become desensitised to insulin and do not respond. Injecting insulin is no use. This type of diabetes is usually treated by diet.

HT Insulin helps to **regulate** a person's blood sugar levels by converting excess **glucose** in the blood to **glycogen** in the liver. People with diabetes might need to inject insulin before meals.

Before injecting insulin, a person with diabetes tests the amount of sugar in their blood with a prick test:

- If they have had food containing a lot of sugar then a bigger dose of insulin is required to reduce the blood sugar level.
- If they intend to exercise, then a smaller dose is required as they will use up a lot of sugar (for energy).

Quick Test

1. Give a brief definition of homeostasis.
2. What causes type I diabetes?
3. How does insulin travel around the body?
4. Are the body's reactions to hormones slower or faster than nervous reaction?

Hormone • Insulin • Diabetes

Plant Hormones

Plants, as well as animals, respond to changes in the environment. Plant **hormones** are chemicals that control:

- the growth of shoots and roots
- flowering and the ripening of fruits.

One group of plant hormones called **auxins** move through the plant in solution. They affect the plant's growth by responding to **gravity** (**geotropism**) and **light** (**phototropism**).

Shoots grow:

- towards light (positive phototropism)
- against gravity (negative geotropism).

Roots grow:

- away from light (negative phototropism)
- downwards in the direction of gravity (positive geotropism) to absorb water and provide support for the plant.

Experiment to Show that Shoots Grow Towards Light

1 Cut a hole in the side of a box. Put three cuttings into the box. The cuttings detect light coming from the hole, and will grow towards it.

2 Cut a hole in the side of another box. Put three cuttings with foil-covered tips in the box. These shoots can't detect the light so they grow straight up.

Plant cuttings — Hole

Tin foil — Hole

Growth towards light increases the plant's chance of survival as it can get light for photosynthesis.

HT **Auxin** is made in the shoot **tip**. Its distribution through the plant is determined by light and can, therefore, be unequal. This is what happens when light shines on a shoot:

1 The hormones in direct sunlight are destroyed.

2 The hormones on the shaded side continue to function, causing the cells to elongate (lengthen).

3 The shoot bends towards the light.

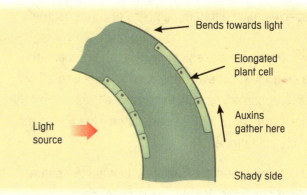

Bends towards light

Elongated plant cell

Light source

Auxins gather here

Shady side

Commercial Uses of Hormones

Plant hormones can be used in agriculture to speed up or slow down plant growth. They include:

- **Rooting powder** – a hormone which encourages the growth of roots in stem cuttings, so many plants can be obtained from one plant.
- **Fruit-ripening hormone** – causes fruit to ripen. Ripening can be accelerated or delayed if required for transportation or storage.
- **Control of dormancy** – hormones can be used to speed up or slow down plant growth and bud development.

- **Selective weedkillers** – hormones in the weedkiller disrupt the growth patterns of their target plants without harming other plants. The broad leaved weeds have a larger surface area than the crop plants with narrow leaves so they receive a bigger dose of hormones and die.

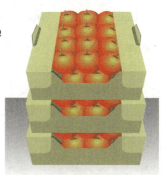

Variation

Differences between individuals of the same species are **variations**. **Genetic** variations occur because individuals **inherit** different combinations of genes. They can be caused by mutations (changes to the genes), differences between individual **gametes** (i.e. eggs and sperm) or the random nature of fertilisation.

Individuals develop in different **conditions**, so some variations are due to **environmental** causes. Some characteristics are determined by a **combination** of genetic and environmental factors.

Genetic	Environmental	Combination
• Nose shape	• Language	• Body mass
• Eye colour	• Scars	• Intelligence
		• Height

HT Scientists are currently debating whether genetics or environment has the greatest influence in the development of characteristics like intelligence, health and sporting ability. It's unlikely that any characteristics are the sole result of one factor.

Alleles

All the instructions to make an individual are held on **chromosomes** kept in the nucleus of all body cells. A section of chromosome which codes for an inherited characteristic or protein is called a **gene**. A person has 23 pairs of chromosomes; different species have different numbers of chromosome pairs. **Gametes** have half the number of chromosomes of normal body cells.

The different versions of genes are called **alleles**. Alleles that control characteristics are described as being **dominant** or **recessive**.

HT **Dominant** alleles control the development of a characteristic even if present on **only one** chromosome in a pair. **Recessive** alleles control the development of a characteristic only if a dominant allele isn't present.

If both chromosomes in a pair contain the **same allele** of a gene, the person is described as being **homozygous** for that gene or condition. If the chromosomes in a pair contain **different alleles**, the person is **heterozygous** for that gene or condition.

When a **characteristic** is **determined** by just **one** pair of alleles, as with eye colour and tongue rolling, it's called **monohybrid inheritance**.

Genetic diagrams are used to show all combinations of alleles and outcomes for a particular gene:
- Capital letters are used for dominant alleles.
- Lower case letters are used for recessive alleles.

For example, for eye colour:
- brown is dominant, so a brown allele is 'B'
- blue is recessive so a blue allele is 'b'.

The letters to describe the genetic make-up are called the **genotype** (e.g. BB) The characteristic expressed is called the **phenotype** (e.g. brown eyes).

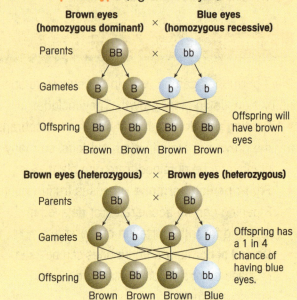

Inheritance of Sex

Gender (in mammals) is determined by the **sex chromosomes**: XX = female; XY = male.
Egg cells all carry X chromosomes. Half of **sperm cells** carry X chromosomes and half carry Y chromosomes.

The sex of an individual depends on whether the egg is **fertilised** by an X- or Y-carrying sperm:

- An egg fertilised by an X sperm will become a girl (X from egg and X from sperm = XX).
- An egg fertilised by a Y sperm will become a boy (X from egg and Y from sperm = XY).

The **chances** of an egg being fertilised by an X-carrying sperm or a Y-carrying sperm are equal, so there are approximately equal numbers of male and female offspring.

HT This genetic diagram shows a 50 : 50 chance of having a boy or girl:

		Male	
		X	Y
Female	X	X X	X Y
	X	X X	X Y

Inherited Diseases

Some diseases are caused by a 'faulty' gene, which means they can be **inherited**. Examples include red–green colour blindness, sickle cell anaemia and cystic fibrosis.

Knowing that there is an inherited disease in a family raises issues, e.g. whether to have children or not, whether to abort an affected foetus.

HT Inherited disorders such as cystic fibrosis are mostly caused by **recessive faulty alleles**. The gene for cystic fibrosis is **recessive**, which means that offspring will only have the disorder if **both** genes are faulty.

This genetic diagram (alongside) shows how the cystic fibrosis gene can be passed on to offspring from two **healthy** parents. (The parents don't have the disease because their dominant genes **protect** them.) It shows that there is a 1 in 4 chance that a child will have cystic fibrosis if both its parents are carriers.

Knowing the likelihood that their child could have cystic fibrosis means parents can make decisions about whether to have a child. But this is a very difficult decision.

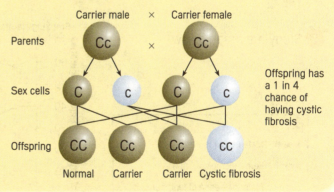

Quick Test
1 What are auxins?
2 Which are the female sex chromosomes – XX or XY?
3 What causes conditions like cystic fibrosis?

1 Louise regularly goes out drinking at the weekends. Explain the short-term effects that the alcohol could have on Louise's body. **[4]**

_____

_____

_____

2 Naveed feels ill and thinks he has a temperature. He thinks his friend at school has given him the flu.

a) Describe how Naveed could measure his body temperature. **[1]**

_____

b) Naveed has a body temperature of 39°C. Could he be ill? Explain your answer. **[2]**

_____

c) In what way does the body prevent microorganisms getting into the lungs? Put a tick (✓) in the box next to the correct answer.

Hydrochloric acid is made ☐   Tears are made ☐   Mucus is made ☐   **[1]**

d) What type of microorganism has caused Naveed's flu? **[1]**

_____

3 **a)** In mammals, gender is determined by sex chromosomes. Which of the following results in a female? Ring the correct answer.

XY   XX   YY   XYY   YXY   **[1]**

b) What are different versions of genes called? **[1]**

_____

4 Study the graph below.

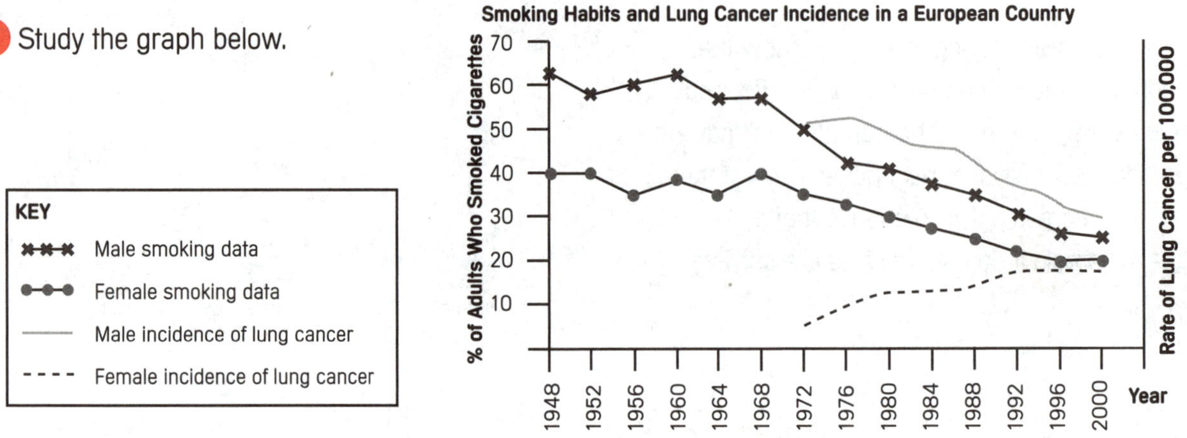

Smoking Habits and Lung Cancer Incidence in a European Country

KEY
✗✗✗ Male smoking data
●●● Female smoking data
—— Male incidence of lung cancer
- - - - Female incidence of lung cancer

a) Describe the pattern of smoking habits since 1972. **[2]**

_____

b) What differences are there in male and female cancer rates? **[2]**

_____

5 This newspaper article gives some information about a new drug.

> **Dieters' dream drug – The Fat Fighter?**
>
> A new drug known as 'ULose' has just been developed that might help people lose weight.
>
> Doctors say that about 11 million people in Britain are obese.
>
> The new drug works by stopping neurotransmitters passing messages between neurones in the brain. This stops people feeling hungry.
>
> Synapses in the brain are affected. Scientists also believe that this drug can help people give up smoking.

a) The new drug may help people to give up smoking. Why is it so hard for people to give up smoking? **[1]**

_____

b) Delroy thinks he might be obese. His body mass is 100 kg and his height is 1.7 metres.

Use this formula to work out if Delroy is obese: $BMI = \dfrac{Mass\ in\ kg}{(Height\ in\ m)^2}$ **[3]**

BMI = _____   Is Delroy obese? _____

Explanation: _____

c) Would Delroy benefit from the new drug? _____ **[1]**

d) Another new drug called 'LJ3' has been developed to help people lose weight. Clinical trials are carried out on ULose and LJ3. The results are shown in the table.

Drug	Number of Volunteers in Trial	Average Weight Loss in 6 Weeks (kg)
LJ3	3250	3.2
ULose	700	5.8
Placebo	2800	2.6

i) In which trial would the data be most reliable? Explain your answer. **[2]**

_____

ii) What conclusion could you draw from the data? **[2]**

_____

iii) Why was a placebo given to some volunteers? **[2]**

_____

HT e) The scientists think that the new drug 'ULose' works because its molecules are similar in shape to the neurotransmitter molecule. Suggest why this stops the passing of messages. **[2]**

_____

_____

6 Ben is running a 10 kilometre race this afternoon. For lunch he decides to have an omelette made of three eggs as he thinks this will provide energy for him in the race later on. Explain whether Ben is correct. **[1]**

_____

B2 Classification

Classification Systems

Classification systems change over time. All living things used to be lumped together into two **kingdoms**: plants and animals. There are now five kingdoms. Living organisms are classified (grouped) according to shared **characteristics**. The five kingdoms are shown in the table.

Kingdom	Features	Feeding Method	Movement
Protista / Protoctista	Single-celled, have a nucleus, some have some chloroplasts, no cell wall, organelles present	Photosynthesis or ingestion of other organisms or both.	Move using cilia or flagella.
Monera (Prokaryotes)	Single-celled, no nucleus, no chloroplasts, have a cell wall	Absorb nutrients through cell wall, or produce their own.	May or may not move.
Fungi	Multicellular, have a nucleus, no chloroplasts, have a cell wall	Acquire nutrients from decaying material.	No mechanisms for movement.
Plants	Multicellular, have a nucleus, chloroplasts and cell walls	Require sunlight to make food through photosynthesis.	Most don't move.
Animals	Multicellular, have a nucleus, no chloroplasts, no cell walls	Acquire nutrients by ingestion.	Move using cilia, flagella or muscles.

HT This classification system may need to be changed in the future as more **species** are found and new discoveries, especially in genetics, are made. Accepted systems of classification have historically changed.

Problems Classifying Organisms

Some organisms from different species can mate and reproduce to give birth to a **hybrid**. Hybrids aren't fertile so they can't be called a new species.

Classifying some organisms, e.g. those in a micro-environment, can be difficult. The variety of life is a continuous spectrum which makes it difficult to place some organisms into distinct groups. Organisms that only reproduce asexually can be hard to classify. Organisms are constantly changing to suit their environment.

Evolutionary Trees

Evolutionary relationships between organisms in the kingdoms can be displayed in **evolutionary trees**.

Monera represent the earliest group of organisms. Monera gave rise to Protista, from which the three other kingdoms of organisms evolved along separate lines. This is a theory that not all scientists agree on.

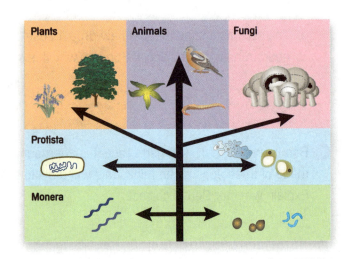

Species

The five kingdoms are divided into **phyla**. Each phylum is divided into **classes**; each class into **orders**; each order into **families**; each family into **genera**; each genus into **species**.

Members of the same species can reproduce together to produce fertile offspring, but within a species there is still lots of **variation**. Each species is given two Latin names, e.g. *Homo sapiens*: this is the **binomial naming system**. Members of a species have more features in common than they do with other organisms of a different species and so tend to live in the same habitat. But, closely related species can be found on different continents where conditions are different so the species may have **evolved** over time to **adapt** to the different conditions. Species **inherit** characteristics so we expect similar species to be closely related to a **common ancestor**.

Species classification takes into account evolutionary relationships as well as ecological relationships.

HT Not all organisms with similar characteristics are descended from a common ancestor. They may have evolved to survive in the same environment so developed similar structures.

For example, whales, dolphins and sharks look quite similar but they're developed from different ancestors. Their similarities are due to sharing a similar environment for millions of years.

HT Artificial and Natural Classification

Artificial classification is based on observed characteristics, e.g. beaks, and is designed for a practical purpose, convenience and simplicity, e.g. **Linnaeus** included all worm-like organisms in a single group; the group included simple nematodes as well as snakes.

Natural classification tries to use natural relationships between organisms. It considers more evidence, including internal and external features. Most classifications today are natural and based on evolutionary relationships.

DNA sequencing has helped with understanding classification. Organisms that are closely related, e.g. brown bears and polar bears have a high degree of DNA sequence similarity.

Arthropods

Invertebrates can be divided into different groups, one of which is the **arthropods**, the largest animal group. Arthropods have limbs with joints that allow them to move, and an exoskeleton, which is shed as they grow. Arthropods are divided into four classes as shown in the table:

Arthropod	Features	Examples
Crustacean	10 or more legs, antennae	Crabs, lobsters
Insect	6 legs, antennae	Dragonflies
Arachnid	8 legs, no antennae	Spiders, mites, scorpions
Myriapod	8–750 legs, antennae	Centipedes, millipedes

B2 Energy Flow

Food Chains

Food chains show the **transfer of energy** from organism to organism. Energy from the Sun flows through a food chain when green plants absorb sunlight to make glucose, and through feeding. Green plants are **producers** because they produce **biomass** during **photosynthesis** (Algae and plankton are other examples of producers). **Consumers** are organisms which eat other organisms. All other organisms in food chains rely on plants.

In ecology, the **trophic level** is the position or stage that an organism occupies in a food chain, what it eats and what eats it.

Biomass and energy are lost at every trophic level of a food chain. Materials and energy are lost in an organism's faeces during **egestion**. Energy is lost through **movement** and **respiration**, especially in birds and mammals, through heat loss and waste (excretion) and so it doesn't go into making new biomass.

Excretory products and uneaten parts can be used as the starting point for other food chains, e.g. dung beetles eating elephant faeces.

Organisms which eat both plants and animals can be both primary and secondary consumers, e.g. humans.

A Food Chain

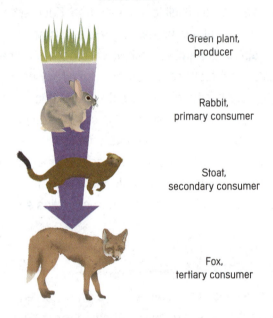

Green plant, producer

Rabbit, primary consumer

Stoat, secondary consumer

Fox, tertiary consumer

HT Efficiency of Energy Transfer

The length of a food chain depends on the **efficiency of energy transfer**. In the food chain above:

- A fraction of the Sun's energy is captured by the producers.
- The rabbits respire and produce waste products. They pass on a tenth of the energy they get from the grass (10%); 90% is lost.
- The stoats respire and produce waste products. They pass on a tenth of the energy they get from the rabbits (10%); 90% is lost.
- The fox gets the last tiny bit of energy left after all the others have had a share.

Food chains rarely have fourth or fifth degree consumers as there isn't enough energy to pass on.

If you know how much energy is stored in the living organisms at each level of a food chain, you can calculate the efficiency of energy transfer:

$$\text{Energy efficiency} = \frac{\text{Energy converted to biomass}}{\text{Total energy taken in}} \times 100$$

Example

A sheep eats 100kJ of energy in the form of grass, but only 9kJ becomes new sheep tissue. The rest is lost as faeces, urine or heat. Calculate the efficiency of energy transfer in the sheep.

$$\text{Energy efficiency} = \frac{9}{100} \times 100 = \textbf{9\%}$$

Producers • Biomass • Photosynthesis • Consumer • Egestion

Food Webs

Food chains link up to make **food webs**. If organisms are removed from, or added to, a food web it has a huge impact on all the other organisms. For example, if the seaweed was removed from this food web, the fish and the winkle numbers may go down due to less food. This may then cause seal and lobster numbers to go down.

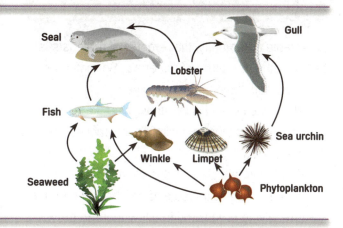

Pyramids of Numbers

The number of organisms at each stage in a food chain can be shown as a **pyramid of numbers**.

The number of organisms decreases as you go up the pyramid, i.e. a lot of grass feeds a few rabbits, which feed even fewer stoats, which feed just one fox.

For simplicity, pyramids of numbers usually look like this:

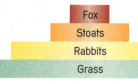

Pyramids of numbers don't take into account the **mass** of the organisms, so it's possible to end up with some odd-looking pyramids. For example, if lots of slugs feed on one lettuce, the base of the

pyramid is smaller than the next stage. This happens because the lettuce is a large organism compared to the slug. This situation also happens when trees are at the bottom of a food chain.

Hawk
Thrushes
Slugs
Lettuce

HT There are problems with creating pyramids of numbers. Some organisms may belong to more than one trophic level and measuring biomass is tricky as it involves drying out and weighing the mass of an organism, which isn't easy with large organisms like trees.

Pyramids of Biomass

Pyramids of biomass show the dry mass of living material at each stage in the chain. They're always pyramid shaped because they take the **mass** of the organisms into account.

Pyramid of Biomass

Quick Test

1. What is a trophic level?
2. Name the four arthropod classes.
3. List the four ways in which energy is lost at each stage of a food chain.
4. **HT** Why is it difficult to classify hybrids?

HT The efficiency of energy transfer **explains the shape of biomass pyramids**. Biomass is lost through the stages. A lot of biomass remains in the ground as the root system. The rabbits and stoats lose biomass in faeces and urine. The fox gets the remaining biomass.

B2 Recycling

Recycling

In a stable community, the removal of materials is balanced by the return of materials. So materials are constantly being recycled:

- When animals and plants **grow**, they **take in** elements from the soil which are incorporated into their bodies.
- When animals **die** and **decay**, these mineral elements are **released** and can be taken up by other living organisms to allow them to grow.

Carbon and **nitrogen** are two recycled elements.

In waterlogged or acidic soils, the recycling of nutrients takes longer. This is because waterlogged soil lacks oxygen for decomposers and acidic soil is not the best pH for decomposers.

The Carbon Cycle

The constant recycling of carbon is called the **carbon cycle**.

1. Carbon dioxide is removed from the atmosphere by green plants for photosynthesis.
2. Plants and animals respire, releasing carbon dioxide into the atmosphere.
3. Soil, bacteria and fungi (**decomposers**) feed on dead plants and animals, causing them to break down, decay and release carbon dioxide into the air. (The **microorganisms** respire as they feed, passing carbon compounds along the food chain.) This decay process makes elements available again to living organisms.

Feeding passes carbon compounds along a food chain. The burning of fossil fuels (combustion) also releases carbon dioxide into the air.

Soil bacteria and fungi are decomposers. They feed on dead animals and plants and then respire, releasing carbon dioxide into the air.

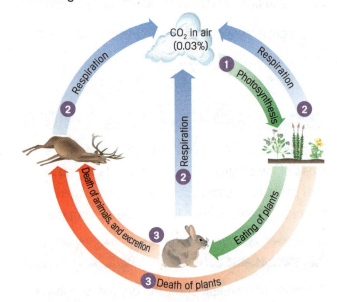

Carbon is also recycled in the sea.

1. Marine organism shells are made of carbonates. The shells drop to the sea bed as the organisms die.
2. The shells fossilise to become limestone rock.
3. Volcanic eruptions heat the limestone and release carbon dioxide into the atmosphere. Carbon dioxide is also released during weathering of the limestone rock.
4. Oceans absorbing carbon dioxide act as **carbon sinks.**

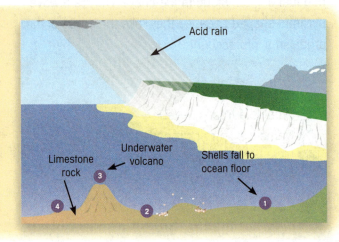

Decay • Decomposers • Microorganism

The Nitrogen Cycle

The air is made up of approximately 78% **nitrogen**. Nitrogen is a vital element used in the production of **proteins**, which are needed for growth in plants and animals. A lot of nitrogen is stored in the air, but animals and plants can't use it because it's so **unreactive**.

The **nitrogen cycle** shows how nitrogen and its compounds are recycled in nature:

1. Plants absorb **nitrates** from the soil to make protein for growth.
2. Animals eat plants and use the nitrogen to make animal protein. Feeding passes nitrogen compounds along a food chain.
3. Dead animals and plants are broken down by decomposers, releasing nitrates back into the soil.

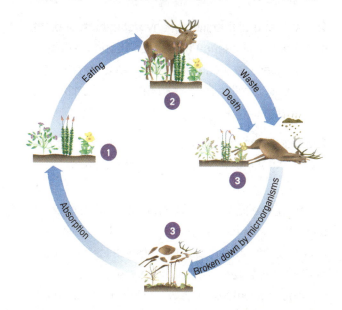

HT The Role of Bacteria

Nitrogen-fixing bacteria convert atmospheric nitrogen into nitrates in the soil. Some of these bacteria live in the soil while others live in root nodules with certain plants (legumes), e.g. peas and beans.

Nitrifying bacteria convert ammonium compounds into nitrates in the soil.

Denitrifying bacteria convert nitrates and ammonium compounds into atmospheric nitrogen.

The energy released by lightning causes oxygen and nitrogen in the air to combine to form nitrogen oxides which dissolve in water. Soil bacteria and fungi act as decomposers, converting proteins and urea into ammonia.

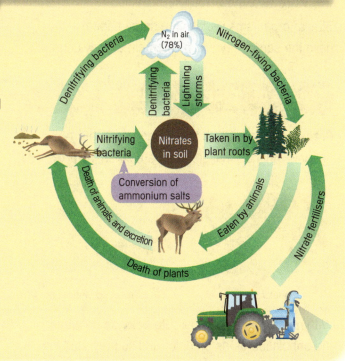

Quick Test

1. Name two recycled elements.
2. How much nitrogen is found naturally in the air?
3. HT Describe the function of nitrifying bacteria.

B2 Interdependence

Competing for Resources

The size and distribution of any **population** of plants or animals will change over time. It can be affected by how well the organisms **compete** for **limited resources**. Similar animals in the same habitat will be in close competition.

Animals compete for food, water, shelter and mates. **Plants** compete for light, water and minerals.

The **better-adapted** competitors will get most of the resources, so they can **survive** and **produce** offspring.

The **interdependence** of organisms determines their distribution and abundance.

HT There are two types of competition: **interspecific** and **intraspecific**. Interspecific competition is where individuals of different species compete for the same resources in an ecosystem, e.g. food or space. Intraspecific competition is where individuals from the same species are competing for the same resource. Intraspecific competition is more significant as these organisms have the exact same needs.

Similar organisms living in the same habitat will have the same prey and nesting sites. They compete to occupy the same **ecological niche** (place and function). They will be in direct competition for the resources they need. For example:

- different ladybird species
- red and grey squirrels.

Red squirrels are the native species to the UK. Grey squirrels were introduced from the USA in 1876, forcing both squirrel species to compete for the same resources. This has led to red squirrels becoming an **endangered** species.

Cycles of Predators and Prey

Predators are animals that kill and eat other animals. Animals that are eaten are called the **prey**.

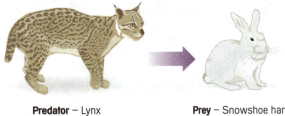

Predator – Lynx   **Prey** – Snowshoe hare

Within nature there's a delicate **balance** between the population of the predator and its prey. But, the prey will always **outnumber** the predators.

There will be **cyclical fluctuations** in the numbers of each species because the numbers of predator and prey will **regulate** each other.

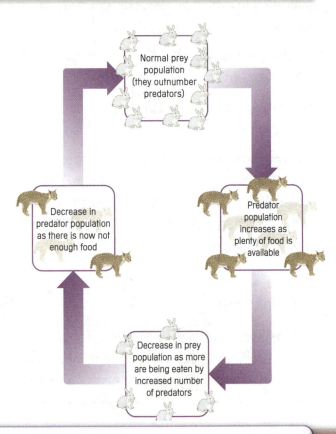

Normal prey population (they outnumber predators)

Predator population increases as plenty of food is available

Decrease in prey population as more are being eaten by increased number of predators

Decrease in predator population as there is now not enough food

HT Cycles of Predators and Prey (Cont.)

When there are lots of hares the lynx have more food so they breed and their numbers go up.

But they then eat lots of hares, so lynx numbers go down. With less food available, the fox numbers go

down. Because it is cause and effect, the peaks and troughs in predator and prey numbers are out of phase.

Parasitic Relationships

Some organisms survive by living off other organisms. They are known as **parasites**, e.g. fleas, tapeworms. The organism they live off is known as the **host** organism.

Parasites can make the host organism ill or even kill it. For example, **tapeworms** (parasites) can be contracted by humans (hosts) by eating pork infected with tapeworm larvae (also known as bladderworms). The tapeworm absorbs food from the person's gut. This can make them very ill.

Flea – a Parasite

Mutualistic Relationships

In **mutualistic** relationships, two organisms form a relationship from which both organisms benefit.

For example, **oxpecker birds** live on **buffalos'** backs.

The oxpecker gets a ready supply of food from the flies and ticks on a buffalo's skin.

The buffalo also benefits as the birds get rid of the pests and provide an early warning system by hissing when lions or other predators approach.

Organisms performing this function, such as oxpecker birds, are known as 'cleaner' species.

HT Another example of a mutualistic relationship can be found in **leguminous plants**, e.g. the pea plant. **Bacteria** in the root nodules take sugars from the plant to use in respiration. They also convert nitrogen into nitrates, which benefits the plant because it enables it to survive in nitrogen-poor soils. So the bacteria gain sugars and the plant gains nitrates.

Buffalo and Oxpecker Bird – Mutualistic Relationship

Quick Test

1. a) What is the term given to organisms that survive by living off other organisms?
   b) Give an example of a mutualistic relationship.
2. HT Name the type of competition which takes place between members of the same species.

Key Words   Parasite • Host • Mutualism

B2 Adaptations

Adaptations

Adaptations are special **features** or **behaviours** that make an organism particularly well **suited** to its **environment**. As plants and animals become better adapted to their environment, they become better able to **compete** for limited **resources**, which enables their **population size** and **distribution** (where they are found) to increase.

If climate changes, those organisms that can successfully adapt to the new conditions will survive.

Adaptations to Cold Environments

Adaptations to very cold environments help organisms to survive. Examples include:

- being well insulated to reduce heat loss
- having a small surface area to volume ratio to prevent heat loss
- behavioural adaptations to help animals to survive cold temperatures, e.g. hedgehogs and groundhogs **hibernate** in winter and birds **migrate** to warmer climates.

The **polar bear** has several adaptations to allow it to survive in a very cold climate:

- Small ears and large bulk reduce surface area to volume ratio to reduce heat loss.
- Large amount of insulating blubber beneath the skin.
- Thick white fur for insulation and camouflage.
- Large feet to spread its weight on snow and ice.
- Fur on the soles of its paws give insulation and grip.
- Powerful legs for running and swimming.

HT Counter-current Heat Exchange Systems

Penguins have a **heat exchange blood flow** to the colder regions. Warm blood entering the feet and flippers flows past cold blood leaving the feet and flippers and warms it up. The warmed up blood re-enters the rest of the body and doesn't affect the penguin's core temperature.

Adaptations to Hot and Dry Environments

Animals in hot environments have behavioural methods of coping with the heat, e.g. finding somewhere cool to go, only going out at night and shedding fur, which all reduce heat gain. Behaviours like taking a swim and panting increase heat loss.

Cacti cope with a lack of water by having long roots to reach water, a thick waxy cuticle to reduce water loss and having spines to reduce water loss and protect water stored in the spongy layer from predators.

Adaptations to Hot and Dry Environments (Cont.)

Camels have several adaptations to allow them to survive in a very hot climate:

- Body fat stored in hump so there's very little insulation under the skin, which keeps it cooler.
- Drinks many litres of water in one go and stores the extra water in the blood.
- Able to tolerate changes in body temperature so doesn't need to sweat very much.

- Hair-lined nostrils trap moisture in its breath before it's exhaled, and the moisture is returned to the body.

Other organisms are also able to trap moisture, for example, desert rats have a long snout-like nose which means they're able to trap moisture to return to the body.

HT Extremophiles

Some organisms are biochemically adapted to extreme conditions. These organisms are called extremophiles. They have enzymes that work at different optimum conditions, e.g. bacteria that live in thermal vents. Some organisms that live in very cold conditions, e.g. some Antarctic fish, possess anti-freeze proteins (AFPs) to prevent ice crystals growing inside tissues.

HT Specialists and Generalists

Some organisms are specialists so are only suited to certain habitats. Other organisms are generalists so they can live in a range of habitats, but can be easily out-competed by other organisms.

Predator and Prey Adaptations

Animals have adapted depending on their position in the food chain, i.e. whether they are predators (and have to chase prey) or prey (who need to escape from predators).

Predators, e.g. lions, polar bears, usually:

- are built for bursts of speed
- are camouflaged to avoid being spotted
- have sharp teeth and claws to grab and kill prey
- have eyes at the front of their head, which provides three-dimensional vision and accurate perception of size and distance (binocular vision)
- have a hunting strategy
- have fewer young than prey animals and give them more care so they survive to adulthood.

Prey, e.g. rabbits, deer, usually:

- are built for speed so they can escape quickly
- are well-camouflaged in their environment – they have cryptic or warning colouration
- live in groups, to increase the opportunities for detecting and confusing predators
- have eyes positioned on the sides of their head for a wide field of view so that they can see predators approaching
- use breeding strategies like synchronous breeding and have more young than predator animals as many get eaten
- use mimicry to protect themselves from predators, e.g. the coral snake's banded pattern is copied by harmless snakes to ward off predators.

B2 Natural Selection

The Theory of Evolution

Animals and plants that are better adapted to their environment are more likely to survive. This theory is called **natural selection** and was first put forward by **Charles Darwin**.

Evolution is the slow, continual **change** of organisms over a very long period to become better **adapted** to their environment. These changes arise through **mutations** (changes in DNA).

These adaptations are controlled by **genes** and can be **passed on** to future generations.

If the environment changes, species must change with it if they are to survive. Animals and plants that are better adapted to their environment are more likely to survive. This is called **natural selection**. Species that aren't well-adapted to their environment may become **extinct**.

Examples of Natural Selection Today

Peppered Moths

Peppered moths can be pale or dark. Pale peppered moths are easily camouflaged amongst the lichens on silver birch tree bark.

But, in areas of high pollution, the bark on silver birch trees is discoloured by soot. In these areas, the rarer, darker speckled varieties of the peppered moth are more common than the pale varieties. This is because the pale peppered moths show up against the sooty bark, whereas the darker peppered moths are camouflaged. So, they're able to survive and breed in greater numbers.

Bacteria and Penicillin

Some **bacteria** have become **resistant** to penicillin by natural selection, as follows:

1. Bacteria mutated. Some were resistant to the antibiotic penicillin; others were not.
2. The non-resistant bacteria were more likely to be killed by the penicillin.
3. The penicillin-resistant bacteria survived.
4. The surviving bacteria reproduce, leading to more bacteria that are resistant to penicillin.

This is why doctors are reluctant to prescribe antibiotics unless they're absolutely necessary.

Natural selection as a theory is now widely accepted.

It explains many observations in nature like the peppered moth. It has also been discussed and tested worldwide by many scientists.

Although the theory of natural selection explains many observations, it doesn't prove that the explanation is correct.

Dark Peppered Moth

Peppered Moth

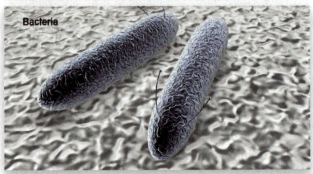

Bacteria

Lamarck's Theory

Lamarck suggested that evolution happened by the **inheritance of acquired characteristics**:

1. Organisms change **during their lifetime** as they struggle to survive.
2. These changes are passed on to their offspring.

Lamarck's theory was **rejected** because there was no evidence that the changes that happened in an individual's lifetime could alter their genes and so be passed on to their offspring. This theory was very different from Darwin's theory and had no genetic basis.

Evolution by Natural Selection

After making extensive observations, **Charles Darwin** proposed his theory of **Evolution by Natural Selection**.

Evolution is the **specialisation** of a population over many generations to become better **adapted** to its environment. There are four key points to remember:

1. Individuals within a population show **natural variation** (i.e. differences due to their genes).
2. There is **competition** between individuals for limited resources (e.g. food, mates) and also predation and disease, which keep population sizes constant in spite of the production of many offspring, i.e. there is a 'struggle for survival', and weaker individuals die.
3. Individuals that are **better adapted** to the environment are more likely to **survive**, breed successfully and produce offspring. This is termed '**survival of the fittest**'.
4. These survivors will therefore pass on their 'successful' **genes** to their **offspring**, resulting in an improved organism being evolved through natural selection.

Species which are unable to compete become **extinct**.

Groups of the same species who are separated from each other by physical boundaries like mountains or seas will not be able to breed and share their genes. This is because over long periods of time, the separate groups may specialise so much that they can't successfully breed any longer and so two new species are formed.

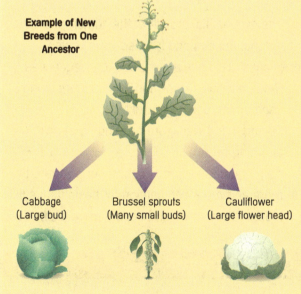

Example of New Breeds from One Ancestor

Cabbage (Large bud)

Brussel sprouts (Many small buds)

Cauliflower (Large flower head)

As new discoveries have been made, and a better understanding of genetics and inheritance is known, the theory of natural selection has been developed and updated.

Many theories have been put forward to explain how evolution may occur. The theory of evolution by natural selection was initially met with hostility. Darwin's ideas went against those of the Church and the Bible. Most scientists now accept the theory put forward by Darwin, but there is still debate amongst some scientists.

Quick Test

1. Who first put forward the theory of evolution?
2. Explain why a species might become extinct or endangered.
3. What organism shows natural selection in action today?
4. HT Why were Darwin's ideas not popular?

B2 Population and Pollution

Pollution

The human population is increasing at a rapid rate. This is the result of the birth rate exceeding the death rate.

This increase in population results in an increase in the demand for **finite** resources, like **fossil fuels** and minerals, which are used for fuel.

As more fossil fuels and oils are burned to produce energy, a greater amount of **pollution** is produced, in particular:

- household waste and sewage
- sulfur dioxide and carbon dioxide.

Pollution can affect the number and type of organisms that can survive. For example, dark peppered moths will survive in polluted areas; pale ones will be eaten as they aren't camouflaged.

Increase in Human Population

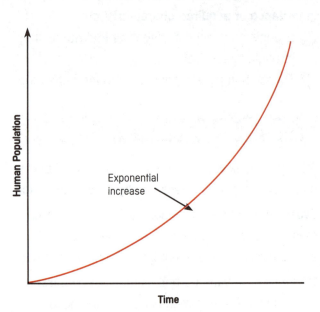

HT The exponential growth of the human population means that the demand for resources is also exponential. This has a number of consequences:

- Raw materials like oil and minerals are being used up increasingly quickly.
- Pollution and waste are building up at an alarming rate.
- As resources become in short supply there is more and more competition for basic things like food and water, which become more expensive.

Although the **developed countries** of the world (e.g. USA, UK, France and Japan) have only a small proportion of the world's population, they use the greatest amount of resources and produce the largest proportion of pollution.

Carbon footprint is the term used to refer to the amount of greenhouse gases a person or event is responsible for emitting in a given timescale. The amount will depend on the person's lifestyle.

Ozone Depletion

Ozone is a **natural gas** found high up in the Earth's **atmosphere**.

It prevents too many harmful ultraviolet (UV) rays reaching the Earth.

Recently, scientists have noticed that the ozone layer is becoming thinner; it is **depleting**. Many people blame the use of **CFCs** (chlorofluorocarbons) in factories, fridges and aerosol cans for this change in the ozone layer. The consequence will be a rise in cases of skin cancer.

Acid Rain

Acid rain is caused by burning fossil fuels which release acid gases like sulfur dioxide and nitrogen oxides. These dissolve in rainwater to make acidic rain. This leads to metals corroding, dissolving of rocks and statues, destruction of forests, and lakes becoming acidic, killing fish and other wildlife.

Fossil fuels • Pollution • **Carbon footprint** • Ozone

Global Warming

The atmosphere keeps the Earth warm; this is known as the **greenhouse effect**:

1. Heat energy from the Sun is reflected from the Earth's surface back out towards space.
2. When it reaches the atmosphere, some rays pass through, but others are trapped in by the carbon dioxide layer. These trapped rays keep the Earth warmer than it would be otherwise, and so allow life to exist.

The amount of carbon dioxide in the atmosphere has increased, which has led to more of the energy being **reflected** back. This is known as **global warming** because the Earth is gradually getting hotter. It may lead to the melting of the polar ice caps, flooding and changes in climate and weather patterns.

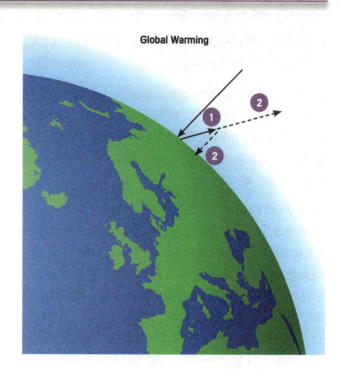

Global Warming

Living Organisms as Indicators

Pollution in the environment can drastically affect the **survival** of living organisms. Some organisms can only cope with 'clean' conditions; they are very sensitive to pollution, so they die. Other species have **evolved** to **resist** the **toxic** effects of pollution so they can **survive**. All these organisms are indicators of pollution and are called **indicator species**. For example, some varieties of lichens are able to survive when high levels of sulfur dioxide are present in the air. The presence of these varieties of lichens acts as an indicator of air pollution.

Some insect larvae, such as the rat-tailed maggot, the bloodworm, the waterlouse and the sludgeworm, can cope with high levels of nitrogen pumped into streams by sewage works outlets. The presence of these organisms is an indicator of water pollution.

Pollution can be measured by using indicator species or by directly measuring pollution levels.

	Advantages	Disadvantages
Using living methods (indicator species)	Reliable, good indicators of long-term effects, easy to identify, cheap, has minimal impact on other organisms.	Seasonal variations, may be killed if pollution is too high, may become diseased and die, organisms may leave the area.
Using non-living methods	Can identify source of pollution, gives quantitative data which can be compared to other locations or time periods.	Expensive as special equipment and chemicals are needed, more people involved.

Quick Test

1. What does sulfur dioxide in the air cause?
2. How are indicator species useful?
3. HT Explain the term 'carbon footprint'.

B2 Sustainability

Sustainable Development

A **sustainable** **resource** is one that can be used and **replaced** so it isn't exhausted (used up completely).

Sustainable development is concerned with ensuring that resources can be used and maintained without compromising the needs of future generations. It's about providing the needs of the population without harming the environment.

Resources can be sustained whilst still being exploited by using **quotas** and ensuring resources are **replenished** or **restocked**, for example, replenishing and restocking pine forests by planting a new sapling for each mature tree cut down. Another example is **conserving** cod stocks:

- The mesh size of fishing nets has been increased to prevent young cod being caught before they reach breeding age.

- Cod quotas have been set to prevent over-fishing.
- Quotas of other fish have been increased.

Education is important so that local people understand the importance of conservation.

HT Exponential increase in human population size makes sustainable development quite a challenge. As the population increases rapidly, the demand for food and energy also increases. The quickest and cheapest ways to meet these demands aren't always the most sustainable.

Sustainability requires planning and **cooperation** at local, national and international levels. Sustainable development can help protect endangered species, e.g. quotas can be set for whaling.

Endangered Species

Endangered **species** are those that are in danger of becoming **extinct** unless something is done to prevent it. The panda and the gorilla are endangered species.

If the number of individuals or their habitats fall below a critical level, the organism is **critically endangered** which means they face an extremely high risk of extinction in the wild. Being critically endangered ranks above being endangered and is one step away from extinction.

The **survival** of plant or animal species can be threatened for a number of reasons, including:

- climate change
- destruction of habitats, e.g. by logging companies, which wipes out food sources and shelter
- hunting
- increased competition for food, shelter, etc.
- pollutants (from pollution) which can accumulate in marine mammals.

If endangered species aren't protected they could become extinct like the mammoth, the dodo and the

sabre-toothed tiger. It is vitally important to conserve endangered species and habitats.

Endangered species can be **protected** by:

- **educating** people about sustainable development
- breeding animals in **captivity** (e.g. zoos) and possibly returning them to their natural habitat to create new populations
- **protecting** (conserving) natural **habitats**
- creating **artificial ecosystems** (e.g. zoos, aquariums) for the species to live in
- **legally protecting** endangered species, so they can't be trapped, killed or kept, except under special licence
- **prohibiting** the **hunting** of legally protected species
- making **seedbanks**.

HT If there isn't enough genetic variation in a population, species become at risk of extinction, e.g. if the organisms are genetically very similar, a disease that kills one may kill them all.

Sustainable • Endangered • Ecosystem

Conservation Programmes

Conservation programmes play an essential role in:

- protecting the human food supply by maintaining the genetic variety of crops, animals and plants
- stabilising ecosystems by ensuring minimal damage to food chains and habitats
- studying and identifying plants which might be useful to develop medicines to treat diseases
- protecting the culture of indigenous people living in threatened habitats such as the Amazonian rainforest.

Whales

Some whale species are now **endangered**, i.e. they are close to extinction. The main causes of whale deaths include:

- becoming entangled in fishing nets and drowning
- being affected by pollutants in the sea
- colliding with ships during migration
- effects of climate change affecting food sources
- culling and hunting.

Money can be made from whales whether they are dead or alive:

- Live whales can be a big tourist attraction.
- Dead whales can be used for food, oil and to make cosmetics.

Whales can be conserved by keeping them in **captivity**, and some zoos have had success with captive breeding. But, captive whales suffer loss of freedom by being reared in a zoo rather than their natural habitat. Often, whales are trained to perform or are used for research purposes.

HT There are many aspects of whale biology that we need to know more about, for example:

- how they communicate over large distances
- how they migrate
- how they dive and survive at extreme depths.

The International Whaling Commission makes **laws** to **protect** whale species and sets quotas for hunting. It's very difficult to enforce these laws though because it's impossible to police all the world's oceans.

It's also difficult to get all countries to agree. Many countries support the idea that whale hunting is unnecessary. But, some countries like Iceland, Norway and Japan disagree with a ban on killing whales. They feel it's necessary to preserve the fishing industry and carry out 'research culls' to investigate the effect of whale population size on fish stocks.

Quick Test

1. **a)** What is meant by the term 'endangered species'?
   b) How can we protect endangered species?
2. What are whales used for (dead and alive)?
3. **HT** Apart from making laws to protect whales, what does the International Whaling Commission do to protect whale numbers?

1 Amelia was listening to the news on the radio when she heard the following headline:

'Cod fishing needs to stop if we are to prevent stocks being virtually wiped out by 2050. However, the UK fisheries minister has ruled out a complete ban on cod fishing, saying that a "zero catch" would see "the end of all fishing in the UK".

a) The fishing industry can protect the cod through sustainable development. One way to sustain the cod is to set quotas. How does setting quotas help to protect the cod? **[1]**

b) It is possible that species like cod could become endangered or even extinct. Suggest two ways in which cod could become extinct, apart from as a result of fishing. **[2]**

2 Look at the picture of a polar bear.

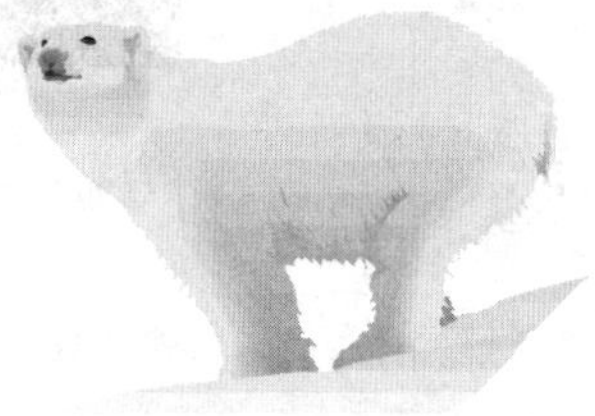

a) Describe and explain two modifications that polar bears have made to adapt to the cold conditions. **[4]**

b) If global warming leads to the melting of polar ice caps, how might this affect the polar bears and why? **[6]**

🖉 *The quality of written communication will be assessed in your answer to this question.*

3 Study each of the following organisms.

    A   B 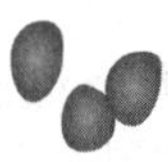   C 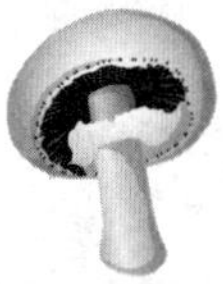   D 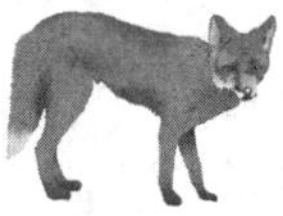   E

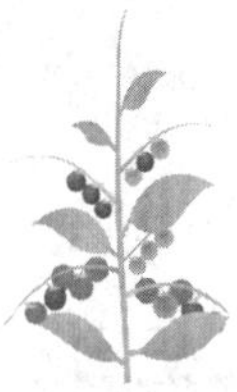

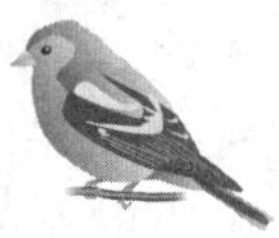

a) Which organism belongs to the fungus kingdom? Explain your answer. [2]

b) Which kingdom does organism **B** belong to? Give a reason for your answer. [2]

c) Another organism, **F**, moves using flagella. Which kingdom does it belong to? [2]

4 The table shows the classification of a number of species.

Kingdom	Phylum	Genus	Species	Common Name
Animal	Equidae	Equus	Zebra	Zebra
Animal	Equidae	Equus	Asinus	Donkey
Animal	Equidae	Equus	Ferus	Horse
Animal	Camelidae	Camelus	Ferus	Camel
Animal	Canidae	Canis	Lupus	Wolf

a) Write down the binomial name for a wolf. [1]

b) Suggest two species which are closely related. Explain your answer. [2]

5 Explain how a cactus is adapted to live in the desert. [4]

HT 6 The length of a food chain depends on the efficiency of energy transfer. Study the food chain below.

Grass ⟶ Grasshopper ⟶ Snake ⟶ Hawk
(70 000kJ)   (12 500kJ)   (2200kJ)   (120kJ)

a) Explain why this food chain does not have fourth or fifth degree consumers. [1]

b) The percentage energy transfer from producer to primary consumer is 17.9%. What is the percentage energy transfer from secondary consumer to tertiary consumer? [2]

B3 Molecules of Life

Cells

Fundamental processes of life take place inside cells. All cells contain the following:

- **Cytoplasm**, where chemical reactions take place.
- A **cell membrane**, which allows movement into and out of the cell.
- A **nucleus**, which contains the genetic information and controls what the cell does.
- **Mitochondria** – **respiration** takes place inside mitochondria, supplying energy for the cell. Cells that have a high energy requirement, e.g. sperm cells, muscle cells and liver cells, have large numbers of mitochondria.

(HT) Some structures are too small to see with a light microscope, e.g. **ribosomes**. Ribosomes are in the cytoplasm and are the site of protein synthesis.

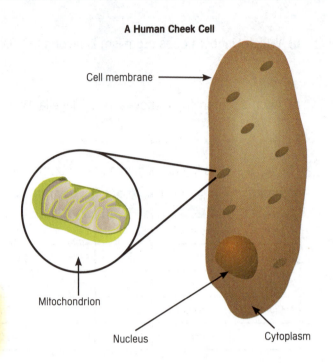

A Human Cheek Cell

Cell membrane

Mitochondrion

Nucleus

Cytoplasm

Genetic Information

Inside the nucleus of every cell are **chromosomes** which carry genetic information in the form of **genes**. A **gene** is a region of chromosome that carries information about, and **controls**, a particular inherited **characteristic**.

The order (or sequence) of the bases provides the **genetic code** (instructions) that controls cell activity. Each gene has a different sequence of bases. The DNA molecules in a cell form a complete set of **instructions** for how the organism should be constructed and how its individual cells should work.

The **nucleus** of each cell contains a complete set of **genetic instructions**. The instructions are carried by **genes** on **chromosomes**. Chromosomes are long coiled molecules of DNA, divided up into regions called genes. Genes are made from a chemical called **DNA** (deoxyribonucleic acid).

Most body cells have the same number of chromosomes, in **matching pairs** – human cells have **23 pairs**.

Gametes (sex cells) contain individual chromosomes and therefore have exactly half the number of normal cells.

DNA Molecule Carries the Genetic Code

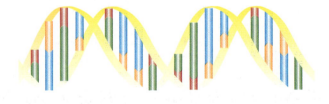

Uncoiled DNA Molecule – The Bases Code for the Protein

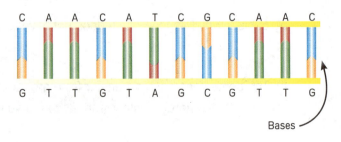

| C | A | A | C | A | T | C | G | C | A | A | C |

| G | T | T | G | T | A | G | C | G | T | T | G |

Bases

Cytoplasm • Nucleus • Mitochondria • Respiration • **Ribosomes** • Chromosome • Gene • DNA • Gamete

DNA

DNA controls the production of proteins. Proteins are needed for growth and repair.

The information in genes is in the form of coded instructions called the **genetic code**. The genetic code controls cell activity and consequently some characteristics of the organism.

A DNA molecule is made of two strands coiled around each other in a **double helix** (spiral). The genetic instructions are in the form of a chemical code made up of four **bases**. These **bases** bond together in specific pairs, forming cross-links.

Each gene contains a different sequence of bases. Genes are like recipes for proteins; each gene codes for a particular protein.

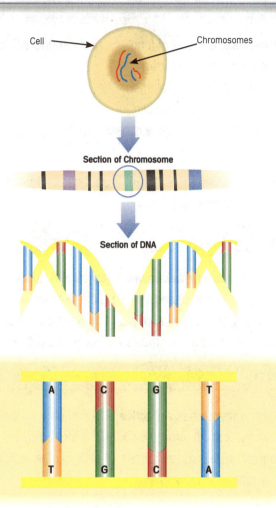

Cell

Chromosomes

Section of Chromosome

Section of DNA

HT The four bases in DNA are **A**, **C**, **G** and **T**.

On opposite strands of the DNA molecule:
- A always bonds with T
- C always bonds with G

This is complementary 'base pairing'.

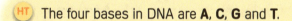

Structure of DNA

The structure of DNA was first worked out by two scientists, **Watson and Crick**. They used data from other scientists to build a model of DNA. X-ray data showed there were two chains wound in a helix and other data indicated that the bases occurred in pairs.

HT New discoveries like Watson and Crick's are not accepted or rewarded immediately. It's important that other scientists can repeat their work and get similar results.

Proteins

Proteins are made in the cytoplasm, but genes can't leave the nucleus so a copy of the gene is needed, which can leave the nucleus.

HT The **sequence of bases** in a gene represents the order in which the cell should assemble amino acids to make the protein. A group of **three bases** represents **one amino acid** in a protein chain. Each protein has a different shape and function.

The code needed to produce a protein is carried from the DNA in the nucleus to the ribosomes in the cytoplasm by a molecule called **mRNA**. DNA controls cell function by controlling the production of proteins, some of which are enzymes.

B3 Proteins and Mutations

Proteins

Proteins are made of long chains of **amino acids**. Their functions include:

- structural, e.g. collagen
- hormones, e.g. insulin
- carrier molecules, e.g. haemoglobin
- enzymes.

Different cells and different organisms will produce different proteins.

> **HT** Each protein has its own number and sequence of amino acids. This results in different shapes of molecule.
>
> It is estimated that there are over 19 000 different proteins in the human body, each with a particular function.

Enzymes

Enzymes are **proteins** which act as biological **catalysts**. They speed up chemical reactions, including those that take place in living cells, e.g. respiration, photosynthesis and protein synthesis.

Enzymes are highly specific. Each one will only speed up a **particular** reaction. Enzyme activity, and therefore the rate of a reaction, can be affected by changes in **temperature** or **pH level**.

The Lock and Key Mechanism

Each **enzyme** has an **active site** that only a specific reactant can fit into (like a key in a lock). High temperatures and extremes of pH stop the lock and key mechanism working.

> **HT** When enzyme molecules are exposed to high temperatures or extreme pH, the following occurs:
> 1. The bonds holding the shape of the protein break.
> 2. The shape of the enzyme's active site is **denatured** (changed irreversibly).
> 3. The 'lock and key' mechanism no longer works.

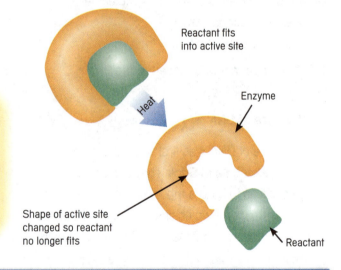

Reactant fits into active site

Enzyme

Heat

Shape of active site changed so reactant no longer fits

Reactant

Enzyme Activity and pH

The graph alongside shows how changes in pH affect enzyme activity. There is an optimum pH at which the enzyme works best. As the pH increases or decreases, the enzyme becomes less and less effective.

> **HT** The active site is damaged irreversibly; the enzyme shape is permanently changed (**denatured**). The lock and key no longer fit.

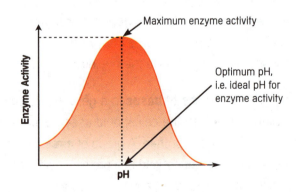

Maximum enzyme activity

Optimum pH, i.e. ideal pH for enzyme activity

Enzyme Activity

pH

Key Words   **Enzyme • Catalyst • Denature**

Enzyme Activity and Temperature

The graph below shows the effect of temperature on enzyme activity:

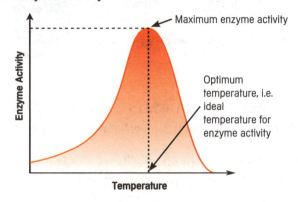

Maximum enzyme activity

Optimum temperature, i.e. ideal temperature for enzyme activity

Enzyme Activity (y-axis)

Temperature (x-axis)

Temperatures above the optimum damage the enzyme molecules irreversibly, decreasing or stopping enzyme activity.

HT This is because the shape is changed (denatured) so the lock and key no longer fit. A rise in temperature increases the frequency of collisions between reactants and enzymes, and will increase the enzyme activity until the optimum temperature is reached. At lower temperatures there are lower collision rates slowing down the rate of the reaction.

Different enzymes have different optimum temperatures. The ones in the human body work best at about 37°C.

HT Measuring the Rate of a Reaction

The rate of an enzyme-controlled reaction can be expressed as a Q_{10} value by comparing the rate at a certain temperature and dividing it by the rate of a temperature 10°C lower:

$$Q_{10} = \frac{\text{Rate at temperature, t}}{\text{Rate at temperature, t} - 10°C}$$

Mutations

Gene **mutations** are changes to **genes**. These changes can be spontaneous, but the rate can be increased by environmental factors such as radiation or chemicals. **Most** mutations are **harmful**, although **occasionally** a **beneficial mutation** occurs. Mutations may lead to production of different proteins.

HT Mutations change the base sequence of **DNA**. This alters the shape and function of the protein or prevents the production of the protein that the gene normally codes for.

Only some of the full set of genes are used in any one cell; some genes are switched off. The genes that are switched on determine the function of the cell.

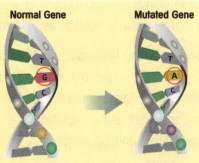

Normal Gene   Mutated Gene

The G base is substituted for an A base

Quick Test

1 Where does respiration take place in a cell?

2 **HT** How do the four bases in DNA pair up?

B3 Respiration

Aerobic Respiration

Energy needed for all life processes in plants and animals is provided by respiration. Life processes require energy from respiration. These include muscle contraction, protein synthesis and control of body temperature in mammals.

Aerobic respiration is the release of energy from glucose in the presence of oxygen. It takes place inside all cells.

During exercise, muscles demand more energy so respiration must go faster to release more energy. Breathing and pulse rate increase to deliver oxygen and glucose to muscles more quickly and remove carbon dioxide from muscles quickly.

To investigate how heart rate responds to exercise, take your resting heart rate. Immediately after exercise, take your heart rate, then take it every minute until it returns to resting. This is the **recovery rate** and is a measure of fitness.

You can compare respiration rates by using the respiratory quotient formula:

$$RQ = \frac{\text{carbon dioxide produced}}{\text{oxygen used}}$$

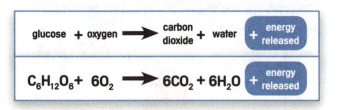

glucose + oxygen → carbon dioxide + water + energy released

$$C_6H_{12}O_6 + 6O_2 \longrightarrow 6CO_2 + 6H_2O + \text{energy released}$$

HT Aerobic respiration requires oxygen and so the rate of oxygen consumption is an estimate of metabolic rate.

Respiration is an enzyme-controlled reaction and so its rate is influenced by pH or temperature.

Respiration results in the production of **ATP**, which is used as the energy source for many processes in cells.

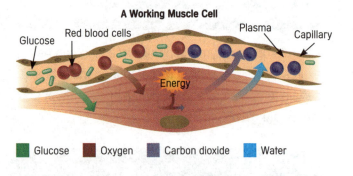

A Working Muscle Cell

Glucose · Red blood cells · Plasma · Capillary · Energy

■ Glucose ■ Oxygen ■ Carbon dioxide ■ Water

Anaerobic Respiration

Anaerobic respiration occurs when your muscles are working so hard that your lungs and circulatory system can't deliver enough oxygen to break down all the available glucose through aerobic respiration.

Anaerobic respiration takes place in the absence of oxygen. It quickly releases a small amount of energy through the **incomplete** breakdown of glucose, so much less energy (about a twentieth) is released than in aerobic respiration.

Lactic acid is produced during anaerobic respiration. It is relatively **toxic** to the cells, and when it builds up in the muscles, it can cause pain (cramp) and a sensation of fatigue in the muscles.

glucose → lactic acid + small amount of energy released

HT During hard exercise there is a lack of oxygen in cells. Incomplete breakdown of glucose occurs. The lactic acid must be broken down quickly to avoid cell damage and relieve the feeling of fatigue.

Immediately after anaerobic exercise:

- **deep breathing continues**, so that oxygen is taken in to break down the lactic acid (producing carbon dioxide, water and more energy).
- the **heart rate stays high**, pumping blood through your muscles to remove the lactic acid and transport it to the liver to be broken down.

In effect, the body is taking in the oxygen that wasn't available for aerobic respiration during exertion. This is why the process is sometimes referred to as 'repaying the **oxygen debt**'.

Key Words   Aerobic respiration • Recovery rate • Anaerobic respiration • Lactic acid

Multi-cell Organisms

Some simple organisms are unicellular, but more complex organisms are multicellular.

Multi-cell organisms (e.g. animals and humans) are **large** and **complex**.

The advantages of being multicellular include:

- allowing organisms to be larger
- allowing for cell differentiation
- allowing organisms to be complex.

HT Becoming multicellular requires the development of specialised organ systems for:

- communication between cells
- supplying the cells with nutrients
- controlling exchanges with the environment.

Cells and Gametes

In mammals, most body cells are **diploid** which means that they contain two sets of matching chromosomes. But, some cells can be **haploid** which means they contain only one set of chromosomes.

Gametes are sex cells (eggs and sperm). They are specialised **haploid** cells. At fertilisation, gametes combine to form a **diploid zygote**. Genetic material from both parents combines to produce a unique individual. Genes on the chromosomes combine to control the characteristics of the zygote.

A **sperm** is a tiny cell with a tail which makes it very mobile. It contains many mitochondria to supply the energy needed for swimming.

On contact with the ovum, its **acrosome** (cap-like structure on its 'head') bursts. This releases enzymes that digest the egg cell's membrane, allowing the sperm nucleus, containing one set of chromosomes from the **father**, to enter. The surface of the egg then changes, making it impossible for other sperm to enter.

Sperm are produced and released in vast numbers because most die on the way so this increases the chance of fertilisation occurring.

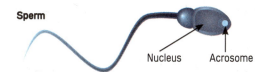

Sperm

Nucleus   Acrosome

Fertilisation

Fertilisation occurs during sexual reproduction. Two gametes (egg and sperm) fuse together.

Sexual reproduction in animals is the joining (fusing) of a sperm and an egg to produce a new, unique

individual. Half the genes come from each parent, as gametes have half the number of chromosomes of body cells.

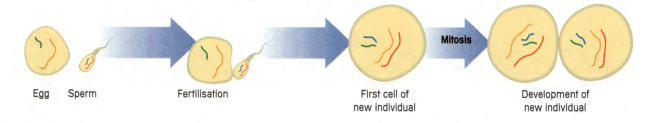

Egg   Sperm   Fertilisation   First cell of   Mitosis   Development of
                                        new individual   new individual

B3 Cell Division

Mitosis

New cells for growth are produced by **mitosis**. These cells are genetically identical. This type of cell division is needed for:

- the replacement of worn-out cells
- repair to damaged tissue
- asexual reproduction.

Before cells divide the DNA copies itself (DNA replication). This means the new cell will have a copy of all the chromosomes. Because there are no other parents involved and the DNA is copied, these cells are genetically identical.

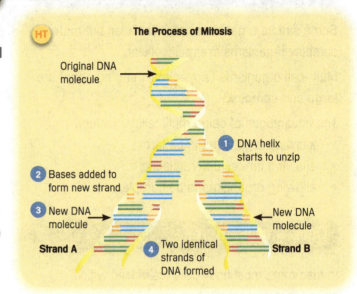

The Process of Mitosis

Original DNA molecule

1. DNA helix starts to unzip
2. Bases added to form new strand
3. New DNA molecule
4. Two identical strands of DNA formed

New DNA molecule

Strand A   Strand B

HT To copy itself, the DNA unzips to form single strands. New double strands form by **complementary base pairing**.

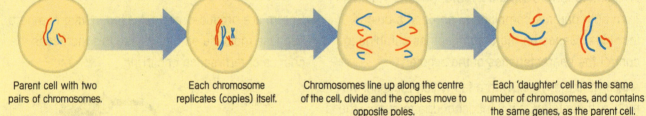

Mitosis – the cell copies itself to produce two genetically identical cells

| Parent cell with two pairs of chromosomes. | Each chromosome replicates (copies) itself. | Chromosomes line up along the centre of the cell, divide and the copies move to opposite poles. | Each 'daughter' cell has the same number of chromosomes, and contains the same genes, as the parent cell. |

Meiosis

Meiosis is a type of cell division which occurs in the testes and ovaries. The cells in these organs divide to produce **gametes** for sexual reproduction.

The chromosome number is halved and each cell is genetically different. Meiosis introduces genetic **variation**.

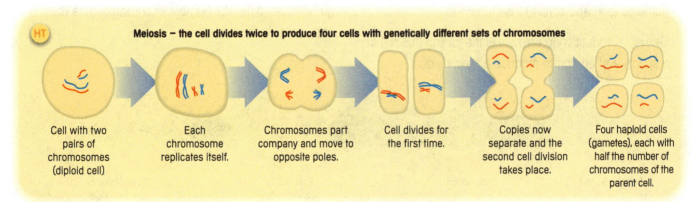

Meiosis – the cell divides twice to produce four cells with genetically different sets of chromosomes

| Cell with two pairs of chromosomes (diploid cell) | Each chromosome replicates itself. | Chromosomes part company and move to opposite poles. | Cell divides for the first time. | Copies now separate and the second cell division takes place. | Four haploid cells (gametes), each with half the number of chromosomes of the parent cell. |

The Blood

Blood has **four** components – platelets (bits of broken cells), plasma, white blood cells and red blood cells.

Platelets clump together when a blood vessel becomes damaged in order to produce a **clot**.

Plasma transports several substances around the body including foods like glucose, water, hormones, antibodies and waste products.

White blood cells protect the body against disease. Some have a flexible shape which allows them to engulf disease-causing microorganisms.

Red blood cells transport oxygen from the lungs to the tissues. They:

- are small and flexible, so they can pass through narrow blood vessels
- don't have a nucleus, so they can be packed with **haemoglobin**.

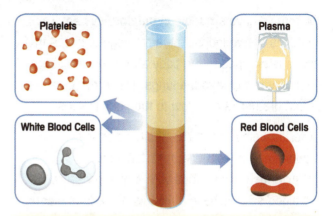

HT The small size and biconcave shape of red blood cells gives them a **large surface area to volume ratio** for absorbing oxygen. When the cells reach the lungs, oxygen diffuses from the lungs into the blood.

The haemoglobin molecules in the red blood cells bind with the oxygen to form **oxyhaemoglobin**.

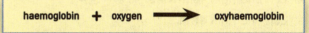

haemoglobin + oxygen ⟶ oxyhaemoglobin

The blood is then pumped around the body to the tissues, where the reverse reaction takes place. Oxygen is released which diffuses into cells.

The Circulatory System

Blood moves around the body in arteries, veins and capillaries:

- **Arteries** transport blood **away** from the **heart.**
- **Veins** transport blood **towards** the **heart.**
- **Capillaries** exchange materials with tissues.

The heart pumps blood around the body:

- The **right hand side** of the heart pumps blood which is low in oxygen **to the lungs and back**.
- The **left hand side** of the heart pumps blood which is rich in oxygen **to the rest of the body and back**.
- Blood pumped into the arteries is under much higher pressure than the blood in the veins.

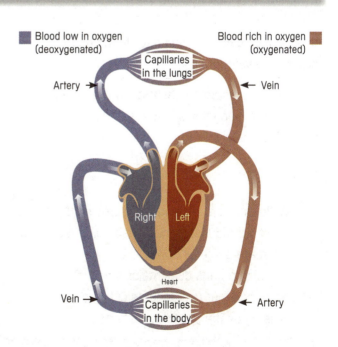

HT The Circulatory System (Cont.)

Mammals have a **double circulatory system**, i.e. it consists of two loops. The advantage of this is that blood is pumped to the body at a higher pressure than it is pumped to the lungs. This provides a much greater rate of flow to the body tissues.

Arteries, veins and capillaries have special adaptations to help with their function:

- **Arteries** have to cope with a high pressure of blood so they have a **thick wall** made of **elastic muscle fibres**.

- **Veins** have a **lumen** which is much bigger compared to the thickness of the walls. They have **valves** to prevent the backflow of blood.
- **Capillaries** are the only blood vessels that have **thin permeable** walls, to allow the **exchange of substances** between cells and the blood.

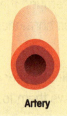  

Artery   **Vein**   **Capillary**

The Heart

Most of the wall of the heart is made of muscle. There are four main chambers:

- Left and right **ventricles**.
- Left and right **atria**.

Ventricles contract to pump blood out of the heart. The right ventricle pumps blood a short distance to the lungs. The left ventricle is **more muscular** because it pumps blood under **higher pressure** around the whole body, whereas the right ventricle only pumps blood to the lungs and back.

Atria receive blood coming back to the heart through the veins.

Semilunar, tricuspid and **bicuspid valves** make sure that the blood flows in the right direction (i.e. not backwards).

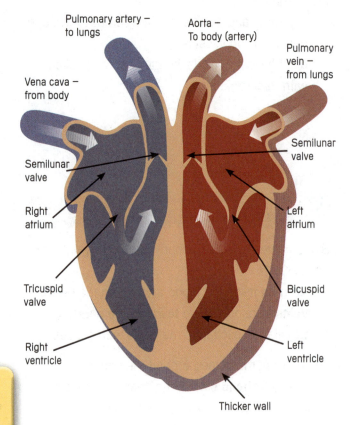

Pulmonary artery – to lungs

Aorta – To body (artery)

Pulmonary vein – from lungs

Vena cava – from body

Semilunar valve

Semilunar valve

Right atrium

Left atrium

Tricuspid valve

Bicuspid valve

Right ventricle

Left ventricle

Thicker wall

Quick Test

1. Write the word equation for aerobic respiration.
2. What is produced during anaerobic respiration?
3. What are gametes?
4. In which organs does meiosis occur?
5. Name the four components of blood.
6. What does the pulmonary artery do?

Plant Cells

Plant and animal cells contain a nucleus, cell membrane, and cytoplasm. Plant cells also contain **chloroplasts**, a **cellulose cell wall** to provide support and a **vacuole** which contains cell sap and helps to provide support.

Use this method to see the parts of a plant cell:

1. Use tweezers to peel a thin layer of skin tissue from an onion.
2. Place the onion tissue onto a microscope slide.
3. Add a drop of iodine to the tissue and carefully cover the slide with a coverslip.
4. Look at the onion cell through the microscope at ×100 magnification.

Bacterial cells are smaller and simpler than plant and animal cells. Bacterial cells lack a true nucleus. They also lack mitochondria and chloroplasts.

HT Plant cells keep their DNA inside the nucleus but bacterial cells have it floating as circular strands.

Palisade Cell (Typical Plant Cell)

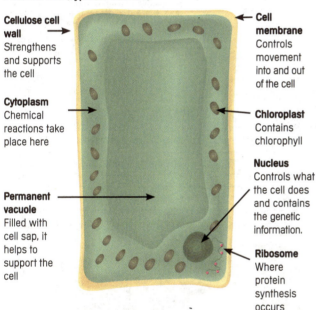

Cellulose cell wall
Strengthens and supports the cell

Cytoplasm
Chemical reactions take place here

Permanent vacuole
Filled with cell sap, it helps to support the cell

Cell membrane
Controls movement into and out of the cell

Chloroplast
Contains chlorophyll

Nucleus
Controls what the cell does and contains the genetic information.

Ribosome
Where protein synthesis occurs

E. coli – An Example of a Flagellate Bacillus

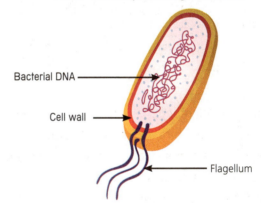

Bacterial DNA

Cell wall

Flagellum

Growth

Growth is measured as an increase in height or mass. It involves both **cell division** and **cell differentiation**. Animals grow by increasing the number of cells. The cells **specialise** or **differentiate** into different types of cell at an early stage to form tissues and organs.

Animal cells lose the ability to differentiate at an early stage. Plant cells do not.

Animals grow in the early stages of their lives, and grow to a finite size. But, given the right conditions, many plants can grow continuously.

All parts of an animal are involved in growth whereas plants grow at specific parts of the plant.

Plant cell division is mainly restricted to areas called **meristems** at the roots and tips.

Cell enlargement is the main method by which plants gain height. Unlike animal cells, plant cells retain the ability to differentiate or specialise throughout their lives, whereas animals lose this ability at an early stage. In humans there are two phases of rapid growth: just after birth and during adolescence.

Apical
Meristem cells located in shoot

Lateral
Meristem cells located in stem

B3 Growth and Development

Growth (Cont.)

Growth Curve

Graph 1 shows the main phases of a typical growth curve for a population. Graph 2 shows a typical growth curve for an individual.

Measuring Growth

Growth can be measured as an increase in length/height, wet mass or dry mass. The best measure of growth is an increase in dry mass.

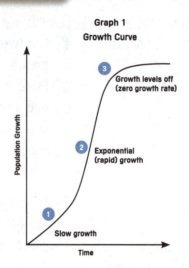

**Graph 1
Growth Curve**

3 Growth levels off (zero growth rate)

2 Exponential (rapid) growth

1 Slow growth

Population Growth

Time

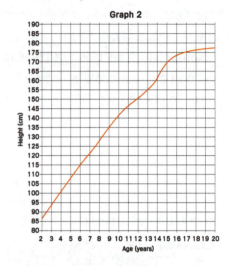

Graph 2

Height (cm)

Age (years)

HT The table below gives a summary of the different ways to measure growth.

Method	Advantage	Disadvantage
Length/height	Easy and rapid measurement.	Increase in mass might occur with no increase in length/height.
Wet mass	Not destructive, is relatively easy to measure.	Water content of living tissue can be very variable and may give a distorted view overall.
Dry mass	Most accurate method.	Destructive as removal of water kills organism.

The growth of different parts of an organism may differ from the growth rate of the whole organism. For example, in a human foetus the head and brain grow rapidly at first to coordinate the complex growth of the rest of the body.

Stages of Development in the Womb

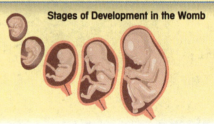

Stem Cells

Stem cells are undifferentiated animal cells, which can specialise and develop into different types of cells, tissues and organs.

Stem cells can be obtained from embryonic tissue and scientists believe that they could potentially be used to treat medical conditions which presently have no cure.

For research, scientists need to obtain large numbers of embryos to grow the stem cells in the laboratory. At present, unused embryos from IVF (*in vitro* fertilisation) treatments are used.

Some people think that embryos left over from an IVF treatment would otherwise be destroyed, so it's a good use for them. The potential to cure disease is important. But others think that it's wrong to experiment on embryos – human life is sacred and shouldn't be experimented on. 'Playing God' is wrong and unnatural.

HT Embryonic stem cells can become any type of body cell, whereas adult stem cells are limited to differentiate into the cell types from their tissue of origin. So, embryonic stem cells have a much wider use.

Selective Breeding

Animals or plants with favourable characteristics are **selected** and **deliberately crossbred** to produce offspring with the desired characteristics. This is selective breeding. These offspring can then also be selected and bred until the desired result is achieved. But, it can take many, many generations to get the desired results.

Selective breeding can contribute to **improved agricultural** yields in animals and crops. For example:

- **Quantity of milk** – cows have been selectively bred to produce **high volumes of milk** daily.
- **Quality of milk** – Jersey cows have been selectively bred to produce **rich** and **creamy milk**.
- **Beef production** – Some cattle have been selectively bred for characteristics such as hardiness, early maturity and high numbers of offspring.

Selective breeding may lead to in-breeding, which can cause health problems within a species.

HT There are risks and disadvantages to selective breeding. Intensive selective breeding reduces the gene pool, and the number of different **alleles** in the population decreases so there is **less variation**. Lack of variation can lead to an accumulation of harmful recessive characteristics (in-breeding).

Example of Selective Breeding

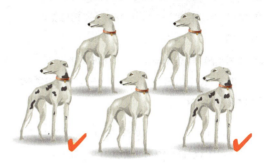

Choose the spottiest two to breed…

… and then the spottiest of their offspring…

… to eventually get Dalmatians.

Genetic Engineering

All living organisms use the same basic genetic code (DNA), so, genes can be artificially transferred from one living organism to another. This process is called genetic engineering or genetic modification (**GM**). The transfer of genes can produce organisms with different characteristics.

Altering the genetic make-up of an organism can be done for many reasons:

- **To improve crop resistance** to frost damage, disease or herbicides, e.g. soya plants are genetically modified by inserting a gene that makes them resistant to a herbicide, so the plants can grow better without competition from weeds.
- **To improve the quality of food**, e.g. people who eat a diet mainly of rice may become deficient in Vitamin A. The genes responsible for producing beta-carotene (which the body converts into vitamin A) can be transferred from carrots to rice plants, so people can get beta-carotene from the genetically modified rice.
- **To produce a required substance,** e.g. the gene for human insulin can be inserted into bacteria to make insulin on a large scale to treat diabetes.

Key Words   **Selective breeding • DNA • Genetic engineering • Genetic modification**

B3 New Genes for Old

Genetic Engineering (Cont.)

Advantage of genetic engineering:
- Allows organisms with new features to be produced rapidly.

Disadvantage of genetic engineering:
- The inserted genes may have **unexpected harmful effects**.

In the future it may be possible to use genetic engineering to change a person's genes and cure certain disorders.

Ethical Considerations

Benefits of genetic engineering/modification include:
- producing disease-resistant crops and higher yields which could feed more of the world's population
- creating crops that will grow in poor or dry soil to feed people in poor areas
- potentially replacing faulty genes to reduce certain diseases.

But, there are concerns that:
- GM plants may cross-breed with wild plants and release their new genes into the environment
- GM foods may not be safe to eat in the long term
- it could lead to the genetic make-up of children being modified or engineered ('designer babies')
- unborn babies with genetic faults could be aborted
- insurance companies could genetically screen applicants and refuse to insure people who have an increased risk of illness.

HT Principles of Genetic Engineering

1. The gene for a desired characteristic is **selected**, e.g. the human insulin gene.
2. The gene is **isolated** and removed using an enzyme which cuts through the DNA strands in precise places.
3. The selected gene is **inserted** into the genome of another organism, e.g. a bacterial cell.
4. When the organism **replicates**, the gene replicates making the new protein, e.g. human insulin.

Gene Therapy

Changing a person's genes in an attempt to cure genetic disorders is called **gene therapy**.

HT Gene therapy can involve body cells or gametes. Gene therapy involving gametes (sex cells, sperm and egg) is very controversial. This is because the genetic changes that are made don't just affect the individual being treated but affect all future generations as those are the genes passed on to the offspring. The future generations don't have a say in the treatment and it may affect them, especially if it leads to problems.

Quick Test

1. Name the process of producing organisms with desired characteristics through a breeding programme.
2. What is gene therapy?
3. How has genetic engineering helped people with diabetes?

Asexual Reproduction

Asexual reproduction produces identical copies. Plants can reproduce asexually, i.e. in the absence of sex cells and fertilisation.

Spider plants, strawberry plants and potato plants all reproduce in this way.

Spider Plant Stolons

Stolon – a rooting side branch

New individual established

New individual (genetically identical) now independent

Taking Cuttings

Plants grown from cuttings or tissue culture are **clones**. If a plant has desirable characteristics, it can be reproduced by taking stem, leaf or root cuttings.

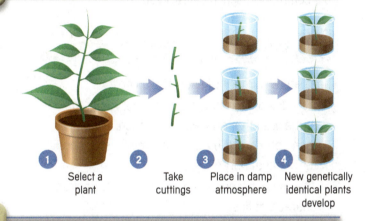

1 Select a plant
2 Take cuttings
3 Place in damp atmosphere
4 New genetically identical plants develop

Commercial Cloning of Plants

Plants can be cloned to be sold commercially.
Advantages include:
* The cloned plants will be genetically identical to the parent, so all the characteristics will be known.
* It is possible to mass-produce plants that may be difficult to grow from seeds.

Disadvantages include:
* Any susceptibility to disease, or sensitivity to environmental conditions will affect all the plants.
* The reduction in **genetic variation** reduces the potential for further selective breeding.

HT Cloning by Tissue Culture

Cloned plants can be produced by the following method:
1 Select a parent plant with desired characteristics.
2 Scrape off a lot of small pieces of tissue into beakers containing nutrients and hormones. Make sure that this process is done **aseptically** (without the presence of bacteria) to avoid the new plants rotting.
3 Lots of genetically identical plantlets will then grow (these can also be cloned).

Many older **plants** are still able to **differentiate** or **specialise**, whereas animal cells lose this ability. So, cloning plants is easier than cloning animals.

B3 Cloning

Cloning Animals

Cloning is an example of asexual reproduction which produces genetically identical copies. Identical twins are **naturally occurring** clones.

Animals can be **cloned artificially**. The most famous example is Dolly the sheep, who was the first mammal to be successfully cloned from an adult body cell.

A cloning technique called **embryo transplantation** is now commonly used in cattle breeding.

Dolly was produced by the process of **nuclear transfer**. This involved scientists placing the nucleus of a body cell (an udder cell) from the sheep they wanted to clone into an empty egg cell, which had had its nucleus removed. A short, sharp electric current helped the cell to start dividing. It was then implanted into another sheep to grow.

Uses of Cloning

There are a number of uses of cloning:

- It's possible to clone human embryos in the same way that animals are cloned. This technique could be used to provide **stem cells** for medical purposes.
- The mass production of animals with desirable characteristics.
- Producing animals that have been genetically engineered to provide human products.

There are major ethical dilemmas about cloning humans:

- The cloning process is very unreliable – the majority of cloned embryos don't survive.
- Cloned animals seem to have a limited life span and die early.
- The effect of cloning on a human's mental and emotional development isn't known.
- Religious views say that cloning humans is wrong.
- Using human embryos and tampering with them is controversial.

HT Adult Cell Cloning

The following method was used to produce a cloned sheep (i.e. Dolly):

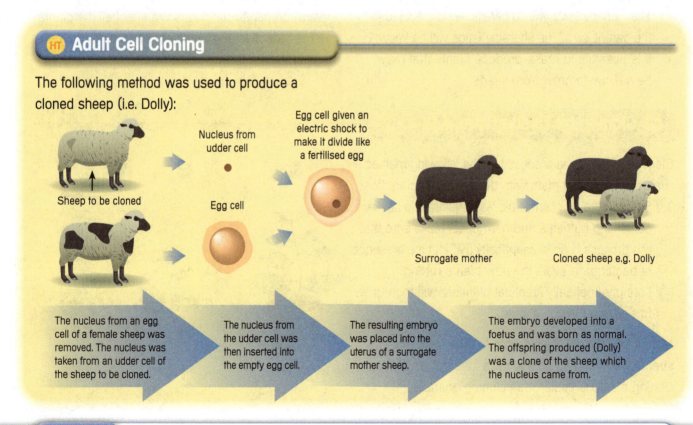

Sheep to be cloned

Nucleus from udder cell

Egg cell

Egg cell given an electric shock to make it divide like a fertilised egg

Surrogate mother

Cloned sheep e.g. Dolly

The nucleus from an egg cell of a female sheep was removed. The nucleus was taken from an udder cell of the sheep to be cloned.

The nucleus from the udder cell was then inserted into the empty egg cell.

The resulting embryo was placed into the uterus of a surrogate mother sheep.

The embryo developed into a foetus and was born as normal. The offspring produced (Dolly) was a clone of the sheep which the nucleus came from.

Key Words   **Embryo • Stem cells**

HT Benefits and Risks of Cloning

There are benefits and risks associated with cloning technology. **Benefits** include:

- Genetically identical cloned animals will all have the same characteristics.
- The sex of an animal and timing of birth can be controlled.
- Top-quality bulls and cows can be kept for egg and sperm donation, whilst other animals can be used to carry and give birth to the young.

Risks include:

- Cloning reduces genetic variation.
- Cloned animals are identical copies so they are all genetically the same. There is potential for one disease wiping them all out.
- Welfare concerns – cloned animals may not be as healthy or live as long as 'normal' animals.

Animal Organ Donors

There is a **shortage** of **human organ donors** for **transplants**.

One possible solution would be to **genetically engineer** (i.e. artificially alter the genetic code of) an **animal** so its organs wouldn't be rejected by the human body. The animal could then be **cloned** to produce a ready supply of identical donor organs.

Animal organ donors could solve the problem of waiting lists for human transplants.
But, there are:

- concerns that infections might be passed from animals to humans
- ethical issues concerning animal welfare and rights.

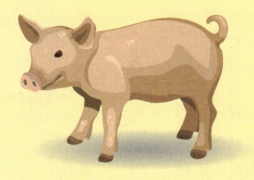 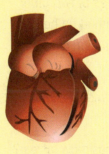 

Quick Test

1. Give an example of naturally occurring clones in mammals.
2. What was the first mammal to be artificially cloned?
3. Suggest some possible uses for cloning.

B3 Exam Practice Questions

1   Look at this diagram of the human heart.

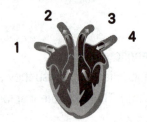

   a) Name the four blood vessels labelled on the diagram.

   1 = ...   2 = ...

   3 = ...   4 = ...   **[4]**

   b) What is the function of the valves?   **[1]**

2   The table shows the number of chromosomes in
    the body cells of a number of animals.

   a) How many chromosomes are in an elephant's sperm cell?   **[1]**

   ....

   b) How many chromosomes are in a mouse's skin cell?   **[1]**

   ....

   c) How does the number of chromosomes in a mouse's body cell compare to the number of
   chromosomes in a human body cell?   **[1]**

   ....

Animal	No. of Chromosomes in Each Body Cell
Elephant	56
Tiger	38
Cat	38
Mouse	40
Carp	104
Snail	24

3   The table on the right charts Thomas's growth
    in mass from birth to age 2.

Age (months)	0	3	6	9	12	15	18	21	24
Mass (kg)	2.8	4.9	6.3	7.4	9.0	9.7	10.0	10.3	10.6

   The graphs show the growth rates of two other
   babies: Gabriel and Finn. Gabriel had no health
   problems from birth to age 2, but Finn did show
   health problems.

   a) Plot a graph of Thomas's growth data and create
   a growth curve.   **[4]**

   b) Between which ages did Thomas grow fastest?   **[1]**

   ....

   c) What can you conclude about Thomas's growth
   from studying the graph?   **[1]**

   ....

   ....

   ....

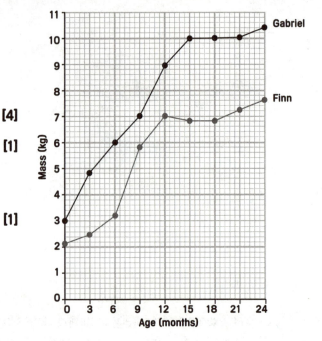

4   The diagram shows the cloning technique that was used to produce Dolly the sheep.

Sheep A   Egg cell

Sheep B

a) What is a clone? _____   [1]

b) Some people do not like the idea of cloning animals. Suggest two reasons why you think this is.   [2]

....

....

c) In nature, give an example you often see of natural clones. ....   [1]

HT d) Describe, with the help of the diagram, the cloning technique shown in the diagram.   [3]

....

....

....

e) Is Dolly a clone of sheep A or B? Without referring to the sheep's colour, explain your answer.   [1]

....

....

5   a) The sequence of bases in DNA determines the order of amino acids in a protein. Here is a sequence of bases for a section of DNA.

A G C T G C T G A C T A

How many amino acids are coded for by this section of DNA?   [1]

....

b) Complete the DNA molecule by adding the correct base to each strand.   [2]

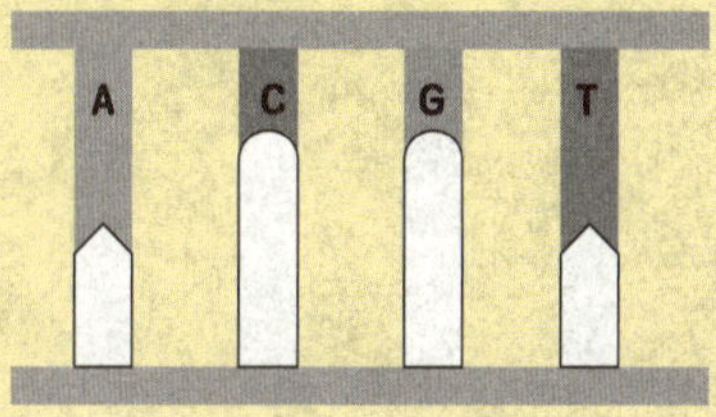

Ecosystems

An **ecosystem** is a physical environment with a particular set of conditions, plus all the organisms that live in it.

An ecosystem can be natural or artificial.

HT **Natural** ecosystems have high **biodiversity**, i.e. many different species of plants and animals **coexist** in the same environment.

Artificial ecosystems, for example, greenhouses, are designed and maintained for a particular **purpose** so they have lower biodiversity.

Weedkillers, **fertilisers** and **pesticides** may be used in artificial ecosystems to prevent other animals and plants from growing alongside the crop. This leads to low biodiversity.

Forestry plantations are very carefully set up, controlled and monitored. They will have less biodiversity due to the fact they haven't been established for as long as natural woodland, which take years to form, and result from the relationships and interactions of the organisms that live there and their surroundings. Fewer species are introduced at the setting up stage and not all species survive from the start.

Fish farms will also show less biodiversity due to the shorter time they have existed compared to lakes. Plus in the absence of many predators some fish species will thrive while others will not. Also there are fewer diseases which may result in too many of certain species reducing others.

Ecological Terms

A **habitat** is the part of the physical environment where an animal or plant lives. An organism will have adapted to its habitat, so it may be restricted to living there. It may only eat the food there.

A **community** is the total number of individuals of all the different populations of plants and animals that live together in a habitat at any one time.

A **population** is the total number of individuals of the same species that live in a certain area.

HT Ecosystems are self supporting in all factors, e.g. providing mates, shelter, but the one thing they all rely on is an energy source (the Sun) and producers at the bottom of the food chain.

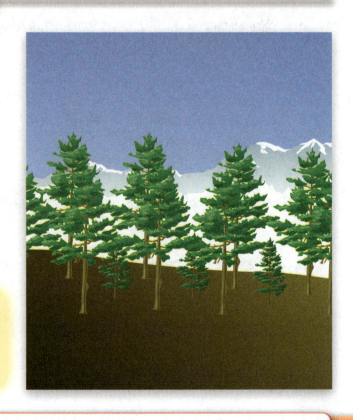

Sampling Methods

The size and distribution of a population can be measured by using one or more of the following techniques: pooters, sweepnets, pitfall traps or quadrats.

Pooters are containers used to collect insects easily, without harming them.

Sweepnets are used to collect insects in long grass or moderately dense woodland where there are lots of shrubs.

Pitfall traps are containers set into the ground that are used to catch small insects, e.g. beetles.

Quadrats are square frames that have sides usually 0.5 m long. They are used to count a smaller, representative part of a population. You should throw them randomly on the ground, then count and record the number of each species within the quadrat. You can then estimate the population of each species in a given area. Quadrat sizes can vary depending on the area you're surveying.

For example, Noah randomly threw 10 quadrats (each quadrat was 0.25 m²) on the school picnic area. He found a total of 2 buttercup plants. So, in 2.5 m² Noah found 2 buttercup plants. The picnic area was 25 m² so **scaling up** would make 20 buttercups on the picnic area. Scaling up is great for estimating a population from a small sample area. It's important that the throws are random.

HT When **sampling**, you must make sure you:
- take a **big enough** sample to make the results a **good estimate** – the larger the sample the more accurate the results
- sample **randomly** – the more random the sample the more likely it is to be **representative** of the population.

In a habitat, organisms are distributed at random.

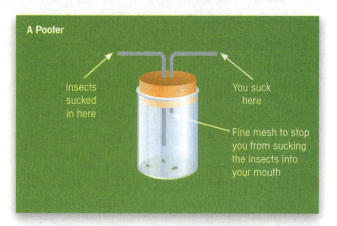

A Pooter

Insects sucked in here — You suck here

Fine mesh to stop you from sucking the insects into your mouth

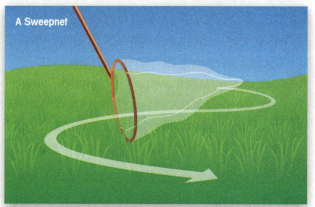

A Sweepnet

A Pitfall Trap

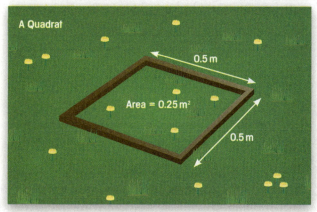

A Quadrat

0.5 m

Area = 0.25 m²

0.5 m

Capture–Recapture

Capture–recapture (also known as the **Lincoln Index**) is a method used to estimate a population size. Populations can be difficult to sample because species move around all the time.

Capture–recapture works as follows:

1. A trap is used to catch a sample of individuals, e.g. mice.
2. The sample is counted and recorded and each individual is marked with a numbered tag/band or a dot of paint.
3. The individuals are released unharmed back into the environment, and are given time to redistribute themselves among the unmarked population.
4. Another sample of individuals is captured. Some of them are already marked and some are unmarked.
5. The unmarked animals are counted and recorded. They are then marked and released.

This formula can then be used to estimate the total population size in the habitat:

$$\text{Population size} = \frac{\text{No. in 1}^{\text{st}}\text{ sample (all marked)} \times \text{no. in 2}^{\text{nd}}\text{ sample (marked and unmarked)}}{\text{No. in 2}^{\text{nd}}\text{ sample which were previously marked}}$$

HT When you use this method you have to:

- assume that no organisms have died, immigrated or emigrated between sampling
- make sure that identical sampling methods are used from one visit to the next
- make sure that marking the organisms doesn't affect their survival, e.g. be careful when using paint on invertebrates because if too much is used it can enter their respiratory passages and kill them.

The larger the sample size, the more accurate the population size estimate.

Using Transects

A **transect** line is used to map the distribution of organisms. It is used for studies of how species change across a boundary between habitats, e.g. a rocky shoreline.

1. A line like a tape measure is laid out.
2. Quadrats are distributed in regular intervals on the line, and the species in the quadrats are counted.

Counting the animals and plants in quadrats along the line of a transect gives a lot of numbers, making it difficult to see trends and compare different parts of the habitat. So the data is presented as a **kite diagram**.

Kite Diagrams

You can create a kite diagram by doing the following:

1 Use graph paper and begin by drawing a sketch of the habitat profile across the bottom to scale.

2 Draw a horizontal line above this and locate the quadrats – mark a vertical bar at each quadrat location (use 5 squares above and 5 below for Abundant, 4 for Common, 3 for Some, 2 for Few, 1 for only one).

3 Join the tops and bottoms of these bars. 'Not present' will be a point on the horizontal line, so the diagram that results will have a shape something like a kite. That is the profile and one species done.

4 Do the same for the next species, and so on.

Remember the presence or absence plus abundance of an organism is affected by other organisms in the area, e.g. predators, as well as other physical factors like the tides or water temperature.

Kite Diagram of Woodland Habitat

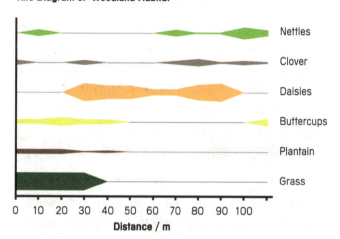

HT

Kite diagrams show **zonation**. Zonation is the gradual change in the distribution of species across a habitat. Gradual changes in abiotic factors (non-living factors), e.g. tides, water temperature, salinity of a rock pool, can result in zonation of organisms in a habitat. This is clearly seen in rocky shores where there are distinct zones of organisms due to the changing tides and the different conditions created.

In the example alongside, zonation of the mussels and periwinkles is directly affected by water level.

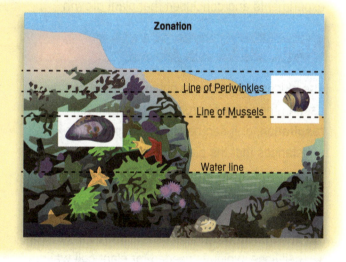

Keys

Correctly identifying species in a sample can be hard. Using keys can help to identify organisms correctly.

Here is an example of a simple key.

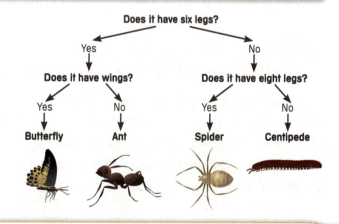

B4 Photosynthesis

Photosynthesis

Green **plants** make their own **food** (glucose and starch), using **sunlight**. This is called **photosynthesis**.

Photosynthesis produces **glucose** for biomass and energy. **Oxygen** is released as a by-product. The equation for photosynthesis is as follows:

$$\text{carbon dioxide} + \text{water} \xrightarrow[\text{chlorophyll}]{\text{light energy}} \text{glucose} + \text{oxygen}$$

$$6CO_2 + 6H_2O \longrightarrow C_6H_{12}O_6 + 6O_2$$

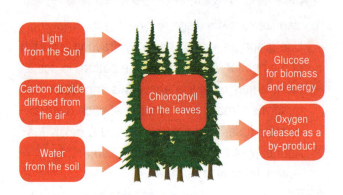

Understanding Photosynthesis

How we understand photosynthesis has changed and evolved over time. The Greek scientists thought that plants gained mass only by taking in minerals from the soil. **Van Helmont** carried out many experiments and concluded that plant growth cannot be due only to the nutrients in the soil.

Joseph Priestley put a plant in a jar of air, and a plant in a jar with a mouse inside. He changed the combinations of plants and mouse and concluded that oxygen is produced by plants.

Using and Storing Food

The glucose produced in photosynthesis can be used immediately to produce energy through **respiration**, or it can be **converted** into other substances that the plant needs. Glucose and starch can be converted into:

- **energy** (during respiration)
- proteins for **growth** and **repair**
- starch, fats or oils that can be **stored** in seeds
- cellulose, which is needed for plant **cell walls**.

Glucose is **soluble**. It can be **transported** around the plant as soluble sugar, but it must be converted into **starch**, which is **insoluble**, in order to be **stored**.

> **HT** Starch is a very useful storage molecule. It is insoluble so it doesn't affect the water **concentration** inside the cells where it's stored. It also does not move away in solution from storage areas. If the cells stored soluble glucose, the inside of the cells would become very concentrated and water would constantly **move** in through osmosis, which would make the cell **swell**.

HT The Chemistry of Photosynthesis

Using radioactive oxygen-18, scientists discovered that the oxygen produced as a by-product in photosynthesis comes from the water and not the carbon dioxide. Only when oxygen-18 is introduced via the water do you get a radioactive waste product of oxygen. This shows that photosynthesis is a two-stage process. Firstly, light energy is used to split water, releasing oxygen gas and hydrogen ions. Secondly, the carbon dioxide gas combines with the hydrogen (ions) to make glucose.

Key Words   **Photosynthesis • Glucose • Soluble • Insoluble**

Increasing Photosynthesis

Plants need **light** and **warmth** to grow. This is why they grow faster in the summer.

Photosynthesis can be **increased** by increasing:

- the **temperature** – using heaters in a greenhouse
- the **light intensity** – using lamps in a greenhouse
- the **carbon dioxide** (CO_2) **concentration** – using chemicals, or as a by-product of using gas heaters in a greenhouse.

HT As the **temperature** rises, so does the rate of photosynthesis. This means temperature is the **limiting factor** in the rate of photosynthesis. As the temperature approaches 45°C, the enzymes controlling photosynthesis start to be denatured and the rate of photosynthesis declines to zero.

As the **carbon dioxide concentration** rises, so does the rate of photosynthesis. So carbon dioxide is limiting the rate of photosynthesis, up to a certain point. After this point, a rise in carbon dioxide levels has no effect. So, carbon dioxide is no longer the limiting factor; light or temperature must be.

As the **light intensity** increases, so does the rate of photosynthesis. This means light intensity is limiting the rate of photosynthesis up to a certain point. After this point, a rise in light intensity has no effect. Light intensity is no longer the limiting factor; carbon dioxide or temperature must be.

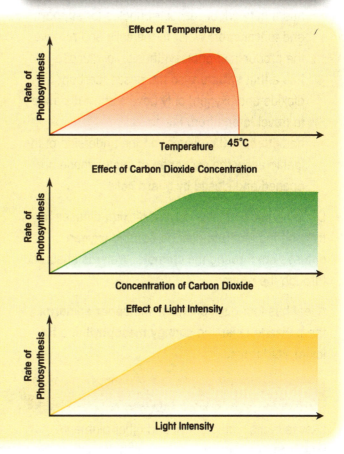

Respiration in Plants

Plants **respire** to break down glucose to release **energy**. They respire all the time, i.e. day and night.

HT During the **day**, light is available from the Sun so plants **photosynthesise**; taking in carbon dioxide to make glucose and releasing oxygen as a by-product.

During the **day** and **night**, they **respire**, absorbing oxygen and giving out carbon dioxide. Respiration is the reverse of photosynthesis. Plants photosynthesise much faster than they respire when light is available. This is why they give out oxygen during the day.

B4 Leaves and Photosynthesis

Plant Leaves

Photosynthesis occurs mainly in the leaves of plants. Leaves are specially adapted for efficiency. For example, a leaf:

- contains a pigment **chlorophyll** (which absorbs light) in millions of chloroplasts, plus other pigments to absorb light from different parts of the spectrum
- is **broad** and **flat** to provide a **huge surface area** to absorb sunlight
- has a network of vascular bundles for **support**, and to **transport** water to the cells and remove the products of photosynthesis, i.e. glucose
- has a **thin structure** so the gases (carbon dioxide and oxygen) only have a short distance to travel to and from the cells
- has **stomata** (tiny pores) on the underside of the leaf to allow the **exchange** of **gases**; these are opened and closed by **guard cells**.

During photosynthesis **carbon dioxide** diffuses in through the **stomata** (leaf pores) and **oxygen** diffuses out through the **stomata**. Water is absorbed through the roots.

A leaf has four distinct layers: the **upper epidermis**, the **palisade layer**, the **spongy mesophyll** and the **lower epidermis**.

Photosynthetic Pigments

Leaves contain chlorophyll and other pigments which absorb different wavelengths of light.

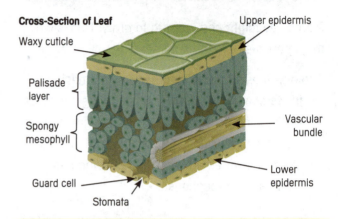

Cross-Section of Leaf

Waxy cuticle · Upper epidermis · Palisade layer · Spongy mesophyll · Vascular bundle · Guard cell · Lower epidermis · Stomata

HT In a typical leaf:

- the **upper epidermis** is **transparent** to allow sunlight through to the layer below
- the **cells** in the **palisade layer** are near the **top** of the leaf and are packed with **chloroplasts** so they can absorb the maximum amount of light
- the **spongy mesophyll** contains lots of **air spaces** connected to the stomata to allow the optimum exchange of gases.

This internal structure provides a **very large surface area** to **volume ratio** for efficient gaseous exchange.

Plant cells contain many chloroplasts and are long so they can absorb lots of light. Chloroplasts are not found in all plant cells, for example, root cells don't have chloroplasts as they obviously don't receive any light.

HT Chlorophyll is a mixture of pigments including chlorophyll a, chlorophyll b, xanthophylls and carotene. This chart shows that when lights of different colours are shone on chlorophyll a and b, they absorb different ranges of colours, but both tend to absorb colours in the red and violet ends of the spectrum. When lights of different colours are shone on a plant and the rate of photosynthesis is measured, the maximum rates are obtained in the red and violet ends too. The greener colours are reflected, which is why plants tend to be green.

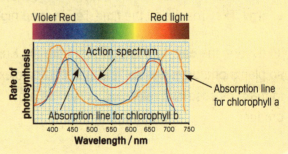

Violet Red · Red light · Action spectrum · Rate of photosynthesis · Absorption line for chlorophyll a · Absorption line for chlorophyll b · 400 450 500 550 600 650 700 750 · Wavelength / nm

Diffusion and Osmosis B4

Diffusion

Substances move in and out of cell membranes by **diffusion**. **Diffusion** is the movement of a substance from a region of **high concentration** to a region of **low concentration**.

Particles move about in lots of different directions. This is called **random movement**. Diffusion is the **net (overall) movement** of particles from an area of high concentration to an area of low concentration.

> **HT** The **rate** of **diffusion** is increased when:
> - there's a greater surface area of the cell membrane
> - there's a greater difference between concentrations (a steeper concentration gradient)
> - the particles have a shorter distance to travel.

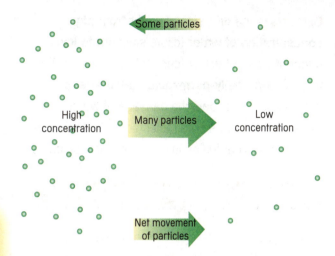

Diffusion in Plants

Carbon dioxide (CO_2) and oxygen (O_2) move in and out of plants through their leaves.

During the day:
- **carbon dioxide** is used up in **photosynthesis**. The concentration inside the leaves is lower than the concentration outside the leaves.
- carbon dioxide diffuses into plants through the stomata (tiny pores) on the bottom of their leaves
- oxygen, a product of photosynthesis, diffuses from the plant into the atmosphere.

At **night**, photosynthesis stops. Oxygen diffuses **into** leaf cells and carbon dioxide diffuses **out of** leaf cells.

The **stomata** on the underside of leaves are specially adapted to:
- **open** – to help increase the rate of diffusion of carbon dioxide and oxygen
- **close** – to prevent excessive water loss in drought conditions.

Magnified Cross-section of Leaf

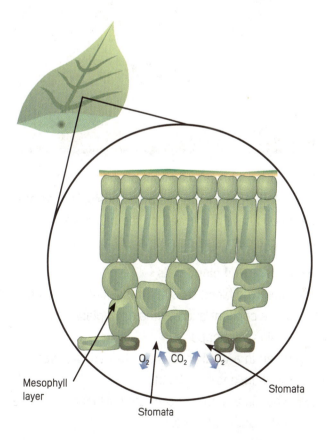

Mesophyll layer

Stomata

Stomata

B4 Diffusion and Osmosis

Osmosis

Osmosis is the **diffusion** of water **from high concentration of water** (dilute solution) **to low concentration of water** (concentrated solution) through a **partially-permeable membrane** (a membrane that allows the passage of water molecules but not solute molecules). Osmosis is a special type of diffusion involving water molecules.

Plant cells are surrounded by a **membrane** which allows water to move in and out of the cells. Water and solute molecules move freely through the cellulose cell wall. The function of the cell wall is to provide support – it doesn't affect the movement of substances in or out of the cell.

HT Net Movement

In osmosis, the water particles move randomly, colliding with each other and passing through the membrane in both directions. But, the **net movement** of molecules is from the area of high water concentration to the area of low water concentration. This gradually **dilutes** the solution.

You can **predict the direction** of water movement if you know what the **concentration** of the water is. Remember, solute molecules can't pass through the membrane; only the water molecules can.

Movement of water is always from high to low water concentration.

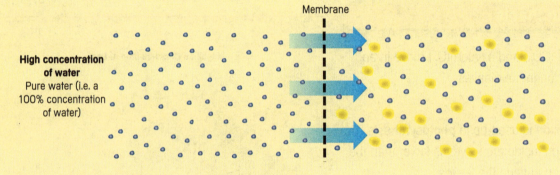

Membrane

High concentration of water
Pure water (i.e. a 100% concentration of water)

Low concentration of water
Sugar dissolved in water, (i.e. less than a 100% concentration of water)

Osmosis in Animal Cells

Water also diffuses in and out of animal cells through the cell membrane by **osmosis**. But, animal cells don't have a cell wall, so too much water entering a cell could cause the cell to burst.

Example – Red blood cells

1. When red blood cells are in solutions with the same concentration as their cytoplasm, they retain their shape.
2. When in a weaker solution, they absorb water, swell up, and may burst.
3. When in a more concentrated solution, they lose water and shrivel up.

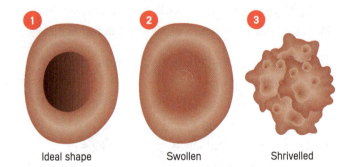

Ideal shape   Swollen   Shrivelled

HT Osmosis in Animal Cells (Cont.)

Animal cells, unlike plant cells, **don't have an inelastic cell wall**.

Blood cells in a pure water solution will gain water by osmosis. Without a cell wall to prevent water entering the cell, they absorb more and more water until eventually they burst. This is called **lysis**.

Blood cells in a concentrated solution (very little water) will lose water by osmosis. Without a cell wall to prevent water loss, they can shrivel up and become **crenated** (have rough edges).

Osmosis in Plant Cells

Plant cells have **inelastic cell walls** which, together with the **water inside the cells**, are essential for the **support** of young non-woody plants. The cell wall:

- prevents cells from bursting due to excess water
- contributes to rigidity.

The pressure of the water pushing against the cell wall is called **turgor pressure**.

A lack of water can cause plants to **droop** (**wilt**). As the amount of water inside the cells reduces, the cells become less rigid due to reduced turgor pressure.

HT As water moves into plant cells **by osmosis**, the **pressure inside the cell increases**. The inelastic cell walls can withstand the pressure and the cell becomes very turgid (rigid). When all the cells are fully turgid, the plant is firm and upright. But, if water is in short supply, cells will start to lose water **by osmosis**. They lose turgor pressure and become flaccid (not rigid), and the plant begins to wilt.

When cells lose a lot of water, the inside of the cell contracts. This is called plasmolysis.

Rigid Plant

Wilting Plant

Quick Test

1. How do gases get in and out of a leaf?
2. Where are stomata found?
3. Which plant cells don't have any chloroplasts?
4. Explain what turgor pressure is and why it's important.

B4 Transport in Plants

Vascular Bundles

The **xylem** and **phloem** form a continuous system of tubes from roots to leaves, called **vascular bundles**.

- **Xylem** transports water and soluble mineral salts from the roots to the leaves (transpiration).
- **Phloem** allows the movement of food substances (sugars) around the plant (translocation), up and down stems to growing tissues and storage tissues.

HT **Xylem vessels** are made from dead plant cells. They have a hollow lumen. The cellulose cell walls are thickened with a waterproof substance. **Phloem** cells are long columns of living cells.

Root hairs have an enormous surface area for absorbing water and so increase the plant's ability to take up water.

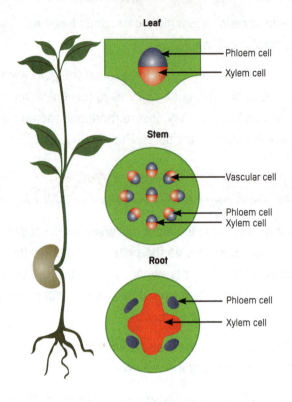

Leaf
- Phloem cell
- Xylem cell

Stem
- Vascular cell
- Phloem cell
- Xylem cell

Root
- Phloem cell
- Xylem cell

Transpiration

Transpiration is the **diffusion** and evaporation of water from inside a leaf. It causes water to be moved up xylem vessels and provides plants with water for cooling, photosynthesis and support, and brings minerals to the plant.

The transpiration stream is powered by the evaporation of water from the leaf:

1. Water evaporates from the internal leaf cells through the stomata.
2. Water passes by osmosis from the xylem vessels to leaf cells, which pull the thread of water in that vessel upwards by a very small amount.
3. Water enters the xylem from root tissues, to replace water which has moved upwards.
4. Water enters root hair cells by osmosis to replace water which has entered the xylem.

The rate of **transpiration** can be affected by:

- **light** – more light increases the rate of photosynthesis and transpiration

- **air movement (wind)** – as the movement of the air increases, transpiration increases
- **temperature** – heat increases the rate of photosynthesis and transpiration
- **humidity** – low humidity increases the rate of transpiration.

A leafy shoot's rate of transpiration can be measured using a **mass potometer**.

1. The plant's roots are submerged in a sealed bag of water and placed in a beaker.
2. The beaker is placed on a digital balance.
3. Readings are then taken to see how much water is lost by the plant during transpiration.
4. The conditions, e.g. light, temperature, can be changed to see how this affects water loss.

Water in Plants

Healthy plants need to balance the amount of water they take in and lose:

1. Water is **absorbed** by the plant by the root hair cells, which have a large surface area to take in water.
2. The water then diffuses through the plant up to the leaves.
3. When it reaches the leaves it can be lost by **transpiration** (evaporation).

Two **adaptations** reduce the rate at which water is lost from leaves:

* A **waxy cuticle** on the surface of the leaf.
* Having the majority of the **stomata** on the **lower surface** of the leaf.

Quick Test

1. What factors affect the rate of transpiration?
2. What is the role of transpiration?
3. HT Describe the structures of the xylem and phloem.

HT Water Loss from Leaves

Transpiration and **water loss** are an unavoidable consequence of photosynthesis. Although **stomata** are **needed** for the **exchange of gases** during photosynthesis, they also allow water molecules to pass out of the leaf. But, the **leaf** is **adapted** to be able to **reduce** water loss:

* The **number**, **position**, **size** and **distribution** of stomata vary between plants, depending on their environment (which affects the amount of water they need).
* The **turgidity** of guard cells changes in relation to the **light intensity** and **availability** of water, in order to alter the size of the stomatal openings.

During photosynthesis, the **guard cells** become **turgid** and the stomata are fully open. But, if there is a lack of water, the guard cells become **flaccid** and the stomata close to prevent unnecessary water loss and photosynthesis. Transpiration rate is affected by:

* **High light intensity** which causes the stomata to open – this increases the rate of water evaporation.

* **High temperatures** which increase the movement of the water molecules – this speeds up transpiration.
* **Increased air movement** which blows the water molecules away from stomata – this increases transpiration.
* **High humidity** which decreases the concentration gradient – this slows down transpiration.

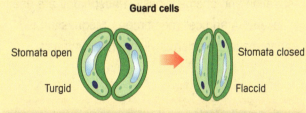

Guard cells

Stomata open — Turgid → Stomata closed — Flaccid

Leaf Adaptation

Spines (leaves adapted to reduce water loss)

Cactus

B4 Plants Need Minerals

Essential Minerals

Essential minerals are needed to keep plants healthy and growing properly. Plants absorb dissolved minerals in the soil through their roots.

The minerals are **naturally present** in the soil, although usually in quite **low concentrations**. So, farmers use fertilisers containing essential minerals e.g. (NPK) to make sure that plants get all the minerals they need to grow.

Each mineral is needed for a different purpose:

- **nitrates (N)** – to make proteins for cell growth
- **potassium compounds (K)** – for respiration and photosynthesis
- **phosphates (P)** – for respiration and cell growth
- **magnesium** – for photosynthesis.

If one or more of the essential minerals is missing (deficient) from the soil, the growth of the plant will be affected.

Experiments can be carried out to see how removing one mineral affects the plants. This is done by growing plants in a soil-less culture. The minerals can then be carefully controlled and changed.

HT **Nitrates** are used to make amino acids that form proteins. **Potassium** is used to help the enzymes in respiration and photosynthesis. **Phosphates** are used to make DNA and cell membranes. **Magnesium** is used to make the chlorophyll for photosynthesis.

Lack of Nitrates
Poor growth, yellow leaves

Lack of Potassium
Poor flower and fruit growth, discoloured leaves

Lack of Phosphates
Poor root growth, discoloured leaves

Lack of Magnesium
Yellow leaves

HT Active Transport

Substances sometimes need to be absorbed from a **low** to a **high concentration** area, i.e. against a concentration gradient. This is called active transport and it requires **energy** from **respiration**.

Plants absorb mineral ions through their root hairs by active transport.

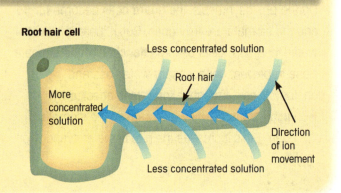

Root hair cell

Less concentrated solution

More concentrated solution

Root hair

Direction of ion movement

Less concentrated solution

Key Words   Fertiliser • Active transport

Decay

Decay is a process involving the breakdown of complex substances into simpler ones by microorganisms. The key factors in the process of decay are microbes, temperature, oxygen and moisture.

The rate of decay is affected by several factors:

- Changing temperature – microorganisms responsible for decay work best at around 40°C.
- Amount of oxygen – microorganisms' rate of activity increases as the amount of oxygen in the air increases.
- Amount of water – microorganisms prefer moist conditions.

HT Temperature – microorganisms work slowly at low temperatures, but at high temperatures (above 40°C) their enzymes are denatured and decay stops.

Amount of oxygen – increasing the amount of oxygen increases the microorganisms' rate of respiration, which means they produce more energy, enabling them to grow and reproduce more quickly. The more oxygen there is, the faster they grow.

Amount of water – microorganisms grow quickest in moist conditions. Too much or too little water will slow down their growth and, therefore, the rate of decay.

Decomposers

Earthworms, woodlice and maggots are known as detritivores. They feed on:

- dead organisms
- decaying material (detritus) produced by living organisms.

Detritivores speed up the process of decay by breaking down detritus into small particles which have a large surface area. This makes it easier for decomposers (bacteria and fungi) to feed on.

Microorganisms are used to break down:

- human waste in sewage treatment works
- plant waste in compost heaps.

Materials that can decay can be recycled because decaying materials release minerals back into the soil. Plants use these minerals to grow.

HT Fungi are saprophytes – they feed on dead organic material by secreting enzymes onto the material and then absorbing the digested products. Saprophytes are essential for decay.

A Garden Composter

B4 Decay

Food Preservation

Food can be preserved by removing the **oxygen**, **warmth** or **moisture** (water) that the microorganisms need in order to grow or survive. Food can be:

- sealed inside sterile cans (canning) – this prevents entry of **decomposers**
- kept at **low temperatures** in a fridge or freezer – this slows down reproduction of the microorganisms' growth
- **pickled** in vinegar – acid kills the decomposers
- **preserved** in sugar (or salt) – this removes water from the decomposers by **osmosis**, so killing them.
- **dried** – this reduces the water.

All these methods reduce the rate of **decay**.

Food Preservation Experiment

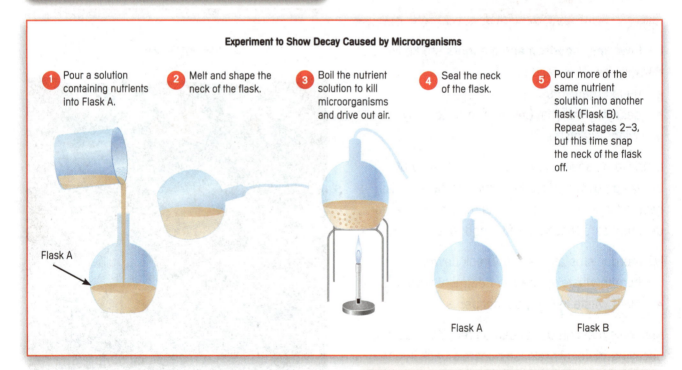

Experiment to Show Decay Caused by Microorganisms

1. Pour a solution containing nutrients into Flask A.
2. Melt and shape the neck of the flask.
3. Boil the nutrient solution to kill microorganisms and drive out air.
4. Seal the neck of the flask.
5. Pour more of the same nutrient solution into another flask (Flask B). Repeat stages 2–3, but this time snap the neck of the flask off.

Flask A

Flask A   Flask B

The solution in the flask that had the neck snapped off (Flask B) will start to decay within days because microorganisms will be able to enter the flask.

But, the solution in the other flask (Flask A) will show no signs of decay as long as it remains sealed.

FROZEN PEAS

MUSHY PEAS

TOMATO SOUP

Farm Fresh Strawberry Jam

Quick Test

1. What does NPK stand for?
2. If a plant lacks nitrates how will it be affected?
3. What is needed for decay?
4. Name six food preservation techniques.

Key Words   **Microorganism • Decomposers • Osmosis**

Intensive Farming

Intensive farming methods aim to produce as much food as possible from the available land, plants and animals. These methods use chemicals like **pesticides** to kill pests that damage crops or livestock so more food is produced:

- **Pesticides** – used to kill pests i.e. any organism that can damage crops or farm animals.
- **Insecticides** (types of pesticide) – used to kill insect pests.
- **Fungicides** (types of pesticide) – used to kill fungi.
- **Herbicides** – used to kill weeds which compete with crops for water and nutrients.

But, care needs to be taken with pesticides because:
- they can harm other organisms (non-pests)
- they can build up (accumulate) in food chains, harming animals at the top.
- some pesticides are persistent – they stay in the food chain for years.

Intensive farming can **increase productivity** by keeping animals in carefully controlled environments where their temperature is controlled and movement is very limited. For example:
- battery farming
- glasshouses
- hydroponics
- fish farming.

But, this can raise **ethical dilemmas**. Some people find this **morally unacceptable** because the animals have a very poor quality of life.

(HT) Keeping animals warm and penned up inside (battery farming) so that they can't move improves the energy transfer by reducing the amount of energy lost at each stage of the food chain. But it's very cruel to the hens as they are kept in such small, confined spaces, and suffer health problems as a result.

By reducing energy transfer to pests, intensive farming improves the efficiency of energy transfer in food chains.

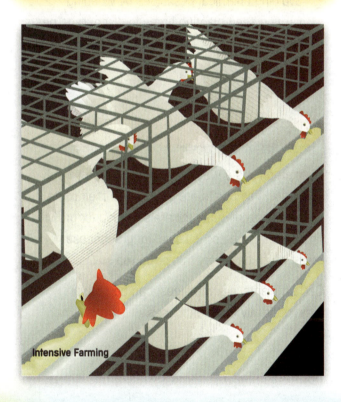
Intensive Farming

Use of Pesticides

B4 Farming

Organic Farming

Organic farming methods aim to produce food without the use of chemicals, so minimising the impact on the environment (no pesticides, no artificial fertilisers).

Organic farming methods include:

- using natural fertilisers like animal manure or compost
- growing nitrogen-fixing crops (e.g. peas or clover)
- rotating crops to maintain soil fertility
- avoiding chemical pesticides by weeding
- varying seed planting times to discourage pests.

Advantages of organic farming:

- Food crops and the environment aren't contaminated with artificial fertilisers or pesticides.
- Soil erosion is limited, and fertility is maintained through the use of organic fertilisers.
- Biodiversity is promoted because hedgerows and other habitats are conserved.
- Livestock have space to roam.

Disadvantages of organic farming:

- It's less efficient because some crops are lost to pests and diseases.
- Organic fertilisers take time to rot and they don't supply a specific balance of minerals.
- It is expensive.
- More space is needed.

Hydroponics

Hydroponics is a way of growing plants without using soil. The plants are grown with their roots in a solution containing the minerals needed for growth. This growing method is useful for **greenhouses** or areas which have very **thin or barren soil**.

Certain plants, e.g. tomatoes, can be grown hydroponically in greenhouses.

HT **Advantages** of hydroponics:

- The mineral levels added to the solution can be carefully controlled and adjusted to the type of plant.
- There is a reduced risk of the plants becoming diseased.

Disadvantages of hydroponics:

- The plants have to be supported as they have no anchorage for their roots.
- Expensive fertilisers are needed to supply the plant with minerals.

Biological Control

Some farmers prefer to **introduce a predator**, instead of using a pesticide, to reduce the number of **pests**. This is called **biological control**.

But, it's important to remember that when biological controls or pesticides are used to get rid of pests, the effect on the rest of the organisms in the food chain or web must be considered.

For example, in the food web shown below, if a pest control was to target rabbits, this would have an effect not only on the rabbits, but also on hawks and foxes (who eat rabbits).

Advantages of biological control:

- The predator selected only usually attacks the pest (i.e. it's species-specific).
- Once introduced, the predator can have an impact over many years, so repeating treatment isn't required.
- The pest can't become resistant to the predator (unlike pesticides).
- No need for chemical pesticides.

Disadvantages of biological control:

- The pest is reduced but it isn't completely removed.
- The predator may not eat the pest or it may even eat useful species.
- The predator may reproduce out of control.
- The predator may leave the area.

Food Web

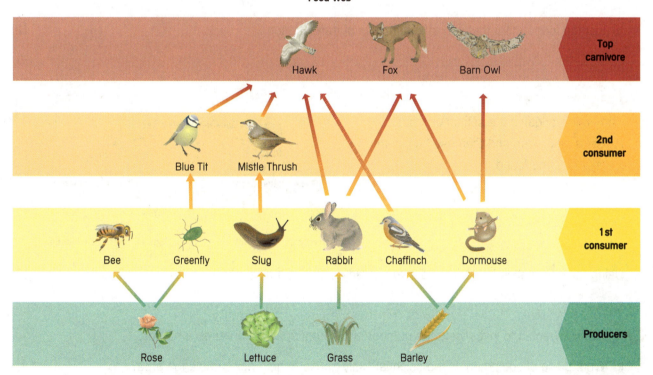

Quick Test

1 Name four intensive farming techniques.
2 Give two disadvantages of organic farming.
3 HT Give two advantages of hydroponics.

1 When Isaac cuts his grass, he puts the grass cuttings in his composter.

a) Name one type of microorganism that causes the grass cuttings to decay. **[1]**

b) Every few weeks, Isaac mixes the compost with a garden fork. Why does he do this and what could happen if he does not? **[4]**

c) Isaac wants to know the best conditions for decay. Ring the best conditions. **[1]**

Warm **Hot** **Cold** **Dry** **Damp** **No oxygen** **Oxygen**

2 The xylem and phloem help transport in plants.

a) What is the function of the xylem? **[2]**

b) List the four factors that can affect the rate of transpiration. **[2]**

1 .... 2 ....

3 .... 4 ....

3 Ahmed investigated the school grounds. He set a pitfall trap and then used a key to identify what he found.

Does it have six legs?
Yes → Does it have wings?
No → Does it have eight legs?
Yes → Butterfly
No → Ant
Yes → Spider
No → Centipede

Using the information in the key, list two characteristics of a butterfly. **[2]**

4 A scientist wanted to investigate the number of different species found on a hillside.

a) What piece of equipment is the scientist likely to use to help her sample the area? **[1]**

b) Describe how the scientist could carry out his investigation. **[3]**

c) A colleague suggests to the scientist that he should have investigated the effect of the slope on the number of species found on the hillside. Suggest a sampling technique that the scientist might use. **[1]**

_____

5 Chloe and James monitored the growth of a number of plants around the school grounds.

They put their data into a table.

	Plant 1	Plant 2	Plant 3	Plant 4	Plant 5
Location of Plant	Playing fields	Edge of car park	Behind library	Edge of car park	Playing fields
Description	Poor growth, yellow leaves	Normal growth, yellow leaves	Normal growth, green leaves	Normal growth, discoloured leaves	Discoloured leaves, underdeveloped flowers

a) What mineral is Plant 1 lacking? _____ **[1]**

b) What mineral is Plant 5 lacking? _____ **[1]**

c) Which location appears to be the best for plants to grow? _____ **[1]**

6 Pierre wanted to investigate osmosis. He cut five equal size potato chips, placed them in five different sugar solutions and left them for 24 hours. He measured the mass of the potato chip before and after the investigation. His results are shown in the table.

Concentration of Sugar Solution (M)	Mass of Potato Chip Before (g)	Mass of Potato Chip After (g)	Difference in Mass (g)
0	1.62	1.74	0.12
0.25	1.72	1.62	0.10
0.5	1.69	1.62	0.07
0.75	1.76	1.6	0.16
1	1.74	1.5	0.24

a) In which concentration did the potato gain mass? _____ **[1]**

b) What caused this gain in mass? **[1]**

_____

c) Suggest how Pierre could increase the reliability of his results. **[1]**

_____

7 Look at this diagram of a palisade cell in a plant.

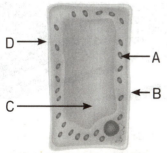

a) One letter shows the vacuole. Which letter is it?
Tick (✓) the correct answer. **[1]**

A ◯   B ◯   C ◯   D ◯

HT b) Explain why the upper epidermis in a leaf is transparent. **[1]**

_____

B5 Skeletons

Types of Skeleton

Animals can have an internal **skeleton**, an external skeleton or no skeleton.

Internal skeletons:
- provide a framework and shape for the body
- grow with the body
- are easy to attach **muscles** to
- have **joints** to allow flexibility.

Some animals including humans have an internal skeleton made mainly from **bone** and **cartilage**, which are **living tissues**. Humans' outer ears, noses and ends of long bones are made of cartilage.

Some animals, such as sharks, have internal skeletons made only of cartilage.

Insects have **external skeletons (exoskeletons)** made from **chitin**. Some organisms, like worms and jellyfish, have soft bodies without hard skeletons.

The advantages of an internal skeleton are that the bones grow with the body, it's easy to attach muscles, and it provides better flexibility.

Long Bones

Long bones have a **hollow shaft**. They weigh less and are stronger than solid bones. The head of the bone is covered in hard, slippery cartilage to lubricate movement against other bones. The shaft contains bone marrow and blood vessels.

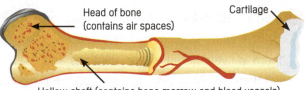
Head of bone (contains air spaces)
Cartilage
Hollow shaft (contains bone marrow and blood vessels)

HT Growing Bones

All the bones in an embryo are made from soft, flexible cartilage. During growth, the cartilage is replaced by calcium and phosphorus salts, which make the bone hard. This is called **ossification**.

Children have cartilage in their bones because they're still growing. Adults only have cartilage at the ends of their bones. Whether a person is still growing or not can be determined by the amount of cartilage present.

Broken Bones

Despite being strong, bones can easily be broken by a sharp knock. X-rays are used to detect fractures in bones. Bones can break or fracture in different ways:
- A **simple fracture** is when the bone breaks cleanly.
- A **greenstick fracture** is when the bone doesn't break completely.
- A **compound fracture** is when the broken bone breaks through muscle and skin.

As people get older, they are more likely to suffer from **osteoporosis**, a condition in which bones are weakened and break more easily.

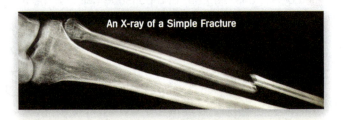
An X-ray of a Simple Fracture

HT It can be dangerous to move someone with a suspected fracture, especially if their spine might be injured, as moving them could make it worse.

Cartilage and bone can get infected if they're damaged. But they can re-grow and repair themselves.

Key Words   Skeleton • Cartilage • Chitin • **Ossification**

Joints

A **joint** is where two or more bones meet. **Ligaments** join bones to other bones.

Muscles contract to make the bones move. **Tendons** attach muscles to bones.

Bony plates are fused together in the **skull**. They're called **fixed joints**.

There are different types of **synovial joint** which allow different types of movement:

- **Hinge joints** (e.g. the elbow, the knee) bend in only one direction.
- **Ball and socket joints** (e.g. the shoulder, the hip) allow rotation.

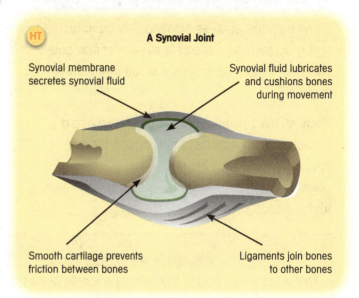

HT

A Synovial Joint

Synovial membrane secretes synovial fluid

Synovial fluid lubricates and cushions bones during movement

Smooth cartilage prevents friction between bones

Ligaments join bones to other bones

Moving the Arm

In the arm the **biceps** and the **triceps** are the main muscles. They're **antagonistic muscles**: when one **contracts**, the other **relaxes**.

1. To bend the arm, the biceps contracts, pulling the radius bone. The triceps relaxes.
2. To straighten the arm, the triceps contracts, pulling the ulna bone. The biceps relaxes.

HT The elbow joint acts as a **pivot**. The biceps muscle is attached close to the elbow so it only contracts a short distance.

The radius bone acts as a lever so the hand moves much further.

A larger distance is moved by the hand than the muscles. A larger force is exerted by the muscles than is exerted by the hand.

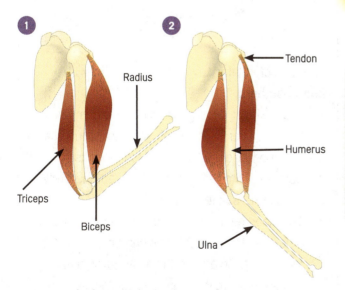

Radius

Triceps

Biceps

Tendon

Humerus

Ulna

Quick Test

1. Name two types of joint.
2. What is meant by antagonistic muscles?
3. **HT** What does the synovial membrane do?
4. **HT** Why is it dangerous to move a person with a suspected fracture?

B5 Circulatory Systems and the Cardiac Cycle

Circulatory Systems

Some animals, such as amoeba, rely on **diffusion** to supply oxygen and nutrients to all parts of their body. This means they don't need a **blood circulatory system**.

Many animals need a blood circulatory system because diffusion alone is not enough for the efficient transfer of materials.

Other animals, such as insects, have an **open circulatory system**. Insect blood isn't contained in blood vessels; it fills up the body cavity.

Some animals, for example, humans, have a **closed circulatory system**. In closed circulatory systems, blood is pumped through vessels called arteries, veins and capillaries.

Single and Double Circulatory Systems

Single Circulatory System	Double Circulatory System
The blood flows around the body in a **single circuit**, for example, in fish.	The blood flows through the heart in **two circuits**, for example, in humans.
Heart ➡ Gills ➡ Body ➡ Heart	Heart ⇌ Lungs Heart ⇌ Body
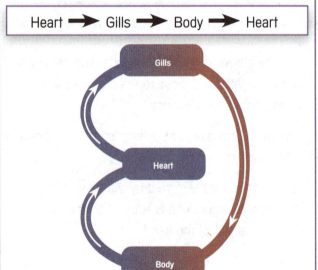	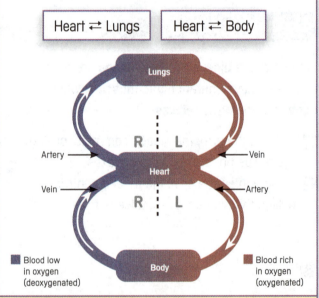 Blood low in oxygen (deoxygenated) Blood rich in oxygen (oxygenated)
(HT) A single circulatory system has a heart with **two chambers**. **Deoxygenated blood** is pumped to the gills, then the **oxygenated blood** is pumped to the body. There is enough pressure to get the blood around the body. Pressure is lower and materials are transported more slowly around the body.	A double circulatory system has a heart with **four chambers**: • In one circuit, deoxygenated blood is pumped from the heart to the lungs and back to the heart. • In the other circuit, oxygenated blood is pumped from the heart to the respiring body cells and back to the heart. • The blood returns to the heart for a further pump otherwise there wouldn't be enough pressure for the blood to go around the body. Blood is under higher pressure in a double circulatory system, so materials are transported more quickly.

The Heart

The **heart** consists of powerful muscles that contract and relax to pump blood around the body. It needs a constant supply of glucose and oxygen to release energy through respiration. The heart never gets tired or needs rest so it has high energy requirements:

- The **coronary artery** supplies the heart itself with glucose and oxygen.
- The **pulmonary vein** carries oxygenated **blood** from the lungs to the heart.
- The **aorta** carries oxygenated blood from the heart to the rest of the body.
- The **vena cava** carries deoxygenated **blood** from the parts of the body back to the heart.
- The **pulmonary artery** carries deoxygenated blood from the heart to the lungs.

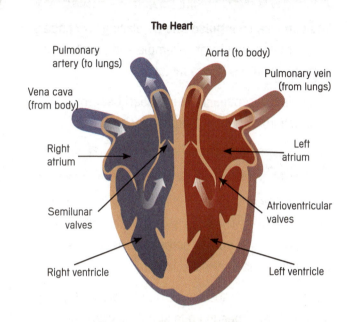

The Heart

HT The Cardiac Cycle

The cardiac cycle is the sequence of events that occurs when the heart beats. During each heart beat:

1. The heart relaxes and blood enters both **atria** from **veins**. The atrioventricular valves are open.
2. The atria contract to push blood into the **ventricles**.
3. The ventricles contract, pushing blood into the arteries. The semilunar valves open to allow this whilst the atrioventricular valves close.

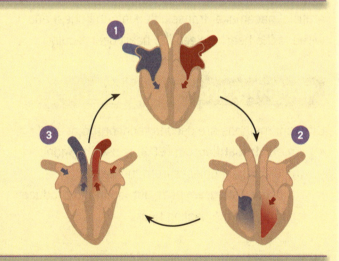

Understanding Circulation

Galen was a Greek doctor who treated gladiators in Rome around 200AD. He believed that blood flowed like a tide between the liver and the heart.

In 1628, **William Harvey**, a British doctor, found that:

- the heart pumped the blood around the body through **blood vessels**
- arteries carried blood under high pressure away from the heart
- veins had **valves** to prevent backflow.

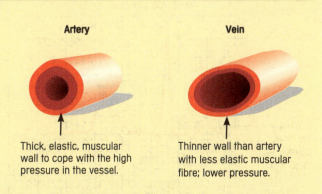

Artery — Thick, elastic, muscular wall to cope with the high pressure in the vessel.

Vein — Thinner wall than artery with less elastic muscular fibre; lower pressure.

Pulse Rate

You can take your **pulse rate** by placing two fingers on your neck, wrist, ear or temple and counting the number of pulses in one minute.

The pulse is a measure of the heart beat (muscle contraction) to put the blood under pressure.

Controlling the Heart Beat

The heart beat is controlled by groups of cells called the **pacemaker**. These cells produce small electrical impulses, which spread across the heart muscle, stimulating it to contract.

During exercise, muscles demand more energy so the heart rate speeds up to supply **oxygen** and **glucose** to respiring muscles more efficiently.

If the pacemaker fails, it's common to have an artificial pacemaker transplanted into the chest and wired to the heart to keep the heart beat regular.

HT The **sinoatrial node** (**SAN**) produces impulses that spread across the atria to make them contract.

The **atrioventricular node** (**AVN**) relays impulses that spread over the ventricles to make them contract.

Nerves connecting the heart to the brain can increase or decrease the pace of the SAN in order to regulate the heart beat.

Hormones, like adrenaline, also alter the heart rate.

Monitoring the Heart

Different methods are used to monitor the heart:

- An **electrocardiogram** (**ECG**) is used to monitor the electrical impulses from the heart.
- An **echocardiogram** uses **ultrasound** to produce an image of the beating heart.

An ECG Electrocardiogram

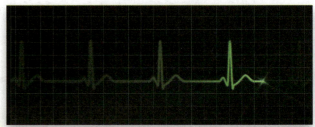

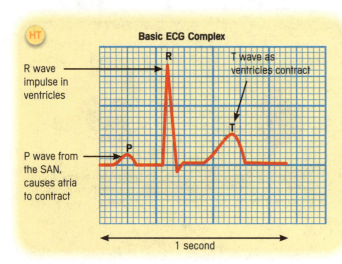

Basic ECG Complex

R wave impulse in ventricles

R

T wave as ventricles contract

T

P wave from the SAN, causes atria to contract

P

1 second

Quick Test

1. Name an organism without a circulatory system.
2. What sort of circulatory system do humans have – open or closed?
3. What is meant by a double circulatory system?
4. HT How do pacemaker cells coordinate heart muscle contractions?

Heart Conditions and Diseases

Irregular heart beat occurs if the pacemaker becomes faulty. An artificial pacemaker can be implanted to restore the regular heart beat.

The cuspid and semilunar **valves can become weak or damaged**, allowing blood to flow backwards and reducing **blood pressure**. Artificial valves can be used to replace them.

The **coronary arteries** that supply the heart with oxygen and glucose can become blocked by fat and **cholesterol**, reducing blood flow to heart muscle and causing a coronary **heart attack** and **coronary heart disease**. **Bypass surgery** uses blood vessels from the leg to replace the blocked arteries.

'Heart-assist devices' are used to help the heart muscles while they recover after a heart attack, as well as heart transplants.

Some people are born with a hole in the heart. This means blood can move from the right side to the left, so oxygenated and deoxygenated blood can mix, resulting in less oxygen in the blood. Surgery can close the hole.

HT A **hole in the heart** is normal in a foetus as they receive oxygen from the mother via the placenta so they don't need a double circulatory system.

At birth, the hole should close. If it doesn't, deoxygenated blood is able to mix with oxygenated blood so the efficiency of transporting oxygen to tissues is reduced.

The hole can be closed using surgery, but it usually closes soon after birth so the baby can have an efficient double system with no mixing of bloods.

Replacement Heart Vs Repaired Heart

Artificial valves or a pacemaker may fix a damaged heart. A severely damaged heart can be replaced by a donor heart.

HT Many factors need to be considered when deciding whether a patient needs a heart **transplant**, pacemaker, or replacement valves fitted.

There are advantages and disadvantages to repairing or replacing the heart.

The advantages of pacemakers and heart valves are:
- There is less risk of rejection.
- They involve a much less traumatic operation.
- Pacemakers and valves can be mechanical, so a human donor isn't needed.
- Shorter waiting time than for a donor heart.
- The patient must take anticoagulants for the rest of their life.

But the disadvantage is:
- They may need replacing.

The advantages of heart transplants are:
- The transplanted organ will last for the lifetime of the patient so it will not need to be replaced.
- The patient will feel better immediately and can lead a full life.

But the disadvantages are:
- It is a major, expensive operation.
- The replacement heart must come from a dead donor.
- There is a long waiting time for a suitable donor (must be right age, size, etc.).
- The patient will need to take immunosuppressants for the rest of their life.

B5 Running Repairs

Blood Clotting

Blood **clots** are nature's way of preventing you from bleeding to death when injured. Blood normally clots at cuts, but sometimes it clots abnormally inside blood vessels.

When you have a cut platelets in the blood gather at the site, forming a clot. This clot prevents further blood loss but it can't do the job forever. A substance called **fibrin** starts to build over the wound. The combination of platelets, fibrin and plasma combine to make a **scab**.

When blood clots abnormally inside blood vessels, **anticoagulant** drugs such as warfarin, heparin and aspirin can be used to reduce clotting.

Haemophilia is an inherited disease where the blood fails to clot due to a faulty clotting protein. Sufferers can bleed to death.

Blood Groups

There are four different **blood groups**: A, B, AB and O. These groups are determined by the A and B markers on the surface of red blood cells.

Rhesus is another marker. There is **Rhesus positive** and **Rhesus negative**.

Each group can be divided into positive and negative.

Blood Donation and Transfusion

Blood **transfusions** save millions of lives. The **National Blood Transfusion Service** collects blood from volunteer blood donors. Donors go to a centre where their blood **haemoglobin** levels are checked. Then, about 500 cm³ of blood is taken from a **vein** in their arm. The blood is screened for diseases and if it's safe it's then stored in sealed packages ready to be transfused into a patient who needs it.

The donor's blood group has to be matched to the recipient's. If it isn't, the donated blood will clump inside the recipient and cause problems.

Many people give blood because they may at one time have had a blood transfusion and know how vital it is. Other people just want to help save lives. It's a quick and simple procedure and it may be the difference between life and death for someone.

HT — Matching Blood Types for Transfusions

Red blood cells have markers called **agglutinins** on their surface, which make them clump if they contact the corresponding antigen.

- A person with blood group A has A-agglutinins.
- A person with blood group B has B-agglutinins.

Unsuccessful blood transfusions can cause agglutination (blood clumping).

Blood Group	Agglutinins on Red Blood Cell Surface	Antibodies Circulating in Blood	Can Accept Blood From...
A	A	Anti-B	A or O
B	B	Anti-A	B or O
AB	A and B	None	Any
O	None	Anti-A and anti-B	O

Key Words   Clot • Anticoagulant • Haemoglobin • Vein • **Agglutinins**

Structures for Gas Exchange

Living organisms must carry out **gas exchange** to get oxygen so they can release energy from food by **aerobic respiration**. Some organisms, such as amoeba and earthworms, are small enough to obtain oxygen by **diffusion** through their moist permeable skin. But bigger, more complex organisms need specialised structures like lungs or gills to obtain oxygen.

Gas Exchange in Fish

Fish have **gills** to obtain oxygen from water. Gills can only function in water so fish can't live out of water. The fish gulps water through its mouth and pushes it out of its gills.

The tadpole stage of an **amphibian** has gills, so it must live and grow in water.

But adult amphibians, such as frogs, use lungs to breathe air so they can live on land. Amphibians need moist habitats as they absorb oxygen through the skin.

HT Fish use gills to exchange gases:
- The oxygen is absorbed by the many fine filaments in the gills.
- The oxygen is transported away from the gill filaments by the blood supply.

Fish can't breathe air because it isn't dense enough to push between the gill filaments. Amphibians can easily lose water through their permeable skin. Both organisms' methods of gas exchange restricts them to their habitat.

Gas Exchange in Humans

The human **thorax** (chest cavity) contains:
- the **trachea** – a flexible tube, surrounded by rings of cartilage to stop it collapsing
- **bronchi** – branches of the trachea
- **bronchioles** – branches of a bronchus
- **lungs** – to inhale and exhale air for gas exchange
- **alveoli** (**air sacs**) – site of gas exchange
- **intercostal muscles** – to raise and lower the ribs
- **pleural membranes** – to protect and lubricate the surface of the lung
- the **diaphragm** – a muscular 'sheet' between the thorax and abdomen.

Oxygen enters the blood in the lungs and leaves the blood in body tissues.

Carbon dioxide enters the blood in body tissues and leaves via the lungs.

The surface area affects the exchange of gases. A large surface area for absorption results in more oxygen being absorbed. Lungs have a huge surface area.

The Lungs

Trachea (windpipe)
Lung
Pleural membrane
Bronchiole
Bronchus (bronchi)
Alveolus (alveoli)
Diaphragm
Rib
Intercostal muscle

B5 Respiratory Systems

Breathing

During **breathing** (**ventilation**), the volume and pressure of the chest cavity are changed by:

- the intercostal muscles
- the diaphragm.

When the intercostal muscles contract, the ribcage moves upwards and outwards. The diaphragm also contracts and flattens. This increases the volume of the chest cavity. The pressure inside the lungs falls, so air rushes in. This is **inspiration**.

When the intercostal muscles relax, the ribcage moves downwards and inwards. The diaphragm also relaxes and moves upwards. This decreases the volume of the chest cavity. The pressure inside the lungs rises, so air is pushed out. This is **expiration**.

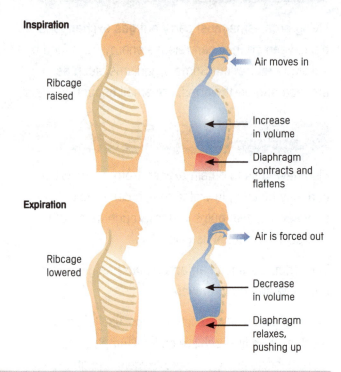

Inspiration
Ribcage raised
Air moves in
Increase in volume
Diaphragm contracts and flattens

Expiration
Ribcage lowered
Air is forced out
Decrease in volume
Diaphragm relaxes, pushing up

Measuring Lung Capacity

Measurements can be taken to calculate lung capacity:

- **Tidal air** is the volume of air breathed in or out in a normal breath.
- **Vital capacity** air is the maximum volume of air that can be used for gas exchange in the lungs – a maximum breath in followed by a maximum breath out.
- **Residual air** is the volume of air that stays in the lungs when we breathe out.

HT The Alveoli

Carbon dioxide diffuses from the blood into the alveoli, and oxygen diffuses from the alveoli into the blood. This is called **gas exchange**. Gas exchange surfaces are well adapted. The alveoli are adapted for gas exchange by having:

- a massive surface area
- a moist, thin, permeable surface
- an excellent blood supply.

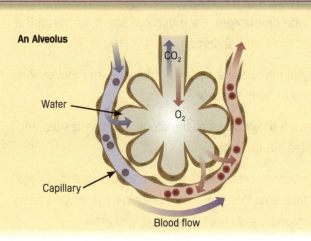

An Alveolus
CO_2
O_2
Water
Capillary
Blood flow

Protection against Disease

The **respiratory system** has defences to protect itself from disease. The **trachea** and **bronchi**:

- produce **mucus** to trap dust and microorganisms
- are lined with millions of **cilia** (ciliated cells) which move the mucus (with dust and microorganisms) from the lungs into the throat, where it's swallowed.

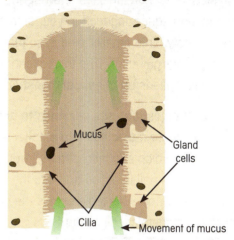

A Breathing Tube in the Lungs

Mucus
Gland cells
Cilia
Movement of mucus

Respiratory Diseases

There are many respiratory (lung) diseases:

- **Asbestosis** is an industrial disease caused by inhaling asbestos fibres. These fibres get trapped in air sacs, reducing gas exchange. It causes excessive coughing, breathlessness and death.
- **Asthma** causes coughing, wheezing, a feeling of tightness in the chest and difficulty breathing. It can be treated using an inhaler containing medicine to relax the bronchiole muscles.
- **Bronchitis** is the inflammation of the bronchi.
- **Cystic fibrosis** is genetically inherited. Too much overly sticky mucus is produced in the lungs, making breathing difficult.
- **Lung cancer** is often caused by lifestyle choices such as smoking. The tar in cigarette smoke causes cells in the lungs to mutate and grow uncontrollably, reducing surface area in the lungs.
- **Pneumonia** is usually caused by a virus or bacterial infection. It causes inflammation in the lungs where fluid builds up.

HT During an asthma attack the lining of the bronchioles becomes inflamed. Fluid and mucus builds up in the airways and the muscles around the bronchioles contract, constricting the airways.

The respiratory system is prone to diseases because the lungs are a 'dead end'.

A Girl with Cystic Fibrosis Using an Inhaler

Quick Test

1. Name four heart conditions.
2. Name the genetic condition where blood does not clot.
3. Name a lung disease which has an industrial cause.
4. Name the blood groups.

B5 Digestion

The Human Digestive System

Physical **digestion** includes chewing food in your mouth, and squeezing food in your stomach to break it down into smaller pieces so that it can pass through your gut easily. The increase in surface area also speeds up **chemical digestion**.

Chemical digestion uses enzymes to break down large insoluble molecules into smaller soluble molecules, which can then **diffuse** through the walls of the small intestine and into the blood plasma or lymph. This table shows the enzymes involved in chemical digestion:

Location	Specific Enzyme	What it Breaks Down
Mouth	• Carbohydrase	• Carbohydrates (e.g. starch into sugars)
Stomach	• Protease	• Proteins into amino acids
Small Intestine	• Carbohydrase • Protease • Lipase	• Carbohydrates into sugars • Proteins into amino acids • Fats into fatty acids and glycerol

Hydrochloric acid is released by cells in the wall of the stomach. It creates the correct pH that helps the enzyme protease to work effectively. The small soluble products of digestion are absorbed into the blood in the small intestine by diffusion.

Absorption in the Small Intestine

Once the large food molecules are broken down into small, soluble molecules they must be absorbed into the bloodstream through the small intestine. The food molecules pass from the small intestine into the blood through the process of diffusion. There is a high concentration of food molecules inside the small intestine but a lower concentration in the blood. The movement of molecules is from a high to a low concentration.

HT The stomach acid provides the optimum pH for the protease enzyme to work, breaking down protein. Other digestive enzymes in the mouth and small intestine have higher optimum pHs.

Your body produces bile to **emulsify** fat droplets, which are hard to digest. The bile breaks down large droplets into smaller droplets to increase their surface area, which enables lipase enzymes to work much faster. Bile comes from the gall bladder to aid digestion.

Starch breaks down in two stages:

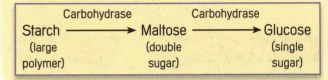

Starch (large polymer) → (Carbohydrase) → Maltose (double sugar) → (Carbohydrase) → Glucose (single sugar)

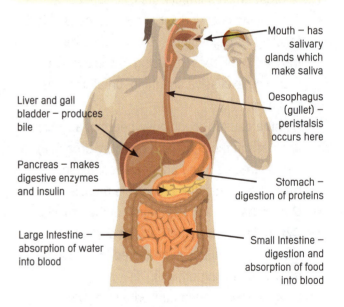

Mouth – has salivary glands which make saliva

Oesophagus (gullet) – peristalsis occurs here

Liver and gall bladder – produces bile

Pancreas – makes digestive enzymes and insulin

Stomach – digestion of proteins

Large Intestine – absorption of water into blood

Small Intestine – digestion and absorption of food into blood

Food enters the blood in the small intestine and leaves in the body tissues.

HT The inside of the small intestine is well adapted for the efficient absorption of food:
*   It is long, and has a thin lining.
*   It has a large surface area provided by villi and microvilli (finger-like projections).
*   It has a permeable surface and rich blood supply.

Digestion • Enzyme • Diffusion • **Emulsify**

Waste Products

Getting rid of solid waste through the anus – mainly undigested food – is called **egestion**.

Getting rid of waste products made by body processes, for example carbon dioxide, urea and sweat, is called **excretion**.

- **Carbon dioxide** is produced by **respiration** and removed by the lungs when you breathe. It is toxic to the body at high levels so must be removed.
- **Urea** is produced from excess **amino acids** broken down in the liver. It's removed by the kidneys.
- **Sweat** is excreted through the skin. The water then evaporates to cool down the skin.

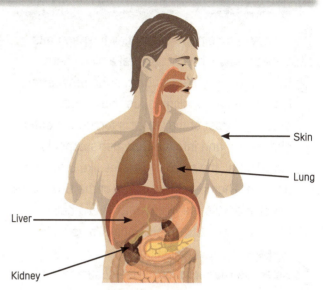

The main organs of excretion are the lungs, kidneys and skin.

Excretion

The volume of **urine** produced is affected by heat and exercise (how much you **drink** and **sweat**):

- If you drink a lot of water, you'll produce a lot of pale, **dilute urine**.
- If you don't drink enough water, or water is lost as sweat during exercise, you'll produce a small amount of **concentrated urine**.

This ensures your body's water content is kept **balanced**.

HT If the brain detects high levels of carbon dioxide in the blood, the breathing rate is increased to remove the excess carbon dioxide.

The Kidneys

It's essential that the right amount of water is maintained in the blood. If there isn't enough water in the blood, you become dehydrated and the blood is thick and difficult to pump. If there's too much water in the blood, your blood pressure could go dangerously high. The amount of water in the blood is controlled by the kidneys.

The kidneys clean the blood. They excrete urea, water and salts. The kidneys contain millions of tiny **tubules** which are very close to the blood capillaries.

The kidneys filter blood at high pressure to separate the small molecules from the blood. They then reabsorb the useful substances, such as sugar and water.

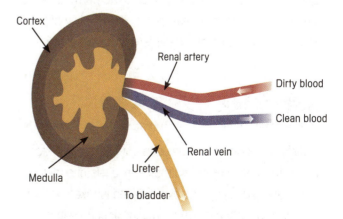

Protein foods are broken down into amino acids. Part of the breakdown results in the production of a poison, urea in the liver. The kidneys remove all of the urea from the blood.

B5 Waste Disposal

HT Kidney Tubules and the Nephron

The kidneys contain millions of tiny filtering units called **nephrons**. Three stages take place here:

1. **Ultrafiltration** – the blood from the renal artery is forced into the glomerulus under high pressure. Most of the water is forced out of the glomerulus and into the Bowman's capsule, including all the small molecules like urea and glucose. The horseshoe shape of the Bowman's capsule allows the glomerulus (a big ball of blood vessels) to sit inside and allows high pressure to be maintained.

2. **Selective reabsorption** – Useful substances like glucose are reabsorbed into the blood, which runs very close by. The coiled up tubule is long and folded to allow time for the useful substances to pass back into the blood.

3. **Salt and water regulation** – The hairpin bend of the Loop of Henlé is where the water is

reabsorbed into the blood. It extends from the cortex to the medulla, allowing plenty of time for reabsorption of water and ions. Complex movements of ions and water across the loop result in the production of concentrated urine.

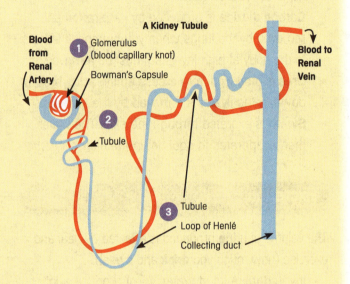

A Kidney Tubule

Blood from Renal Artery

1 Glomerulus (blood capillary knot)

Bowman's Capsule

2

Tubule

3 Tubule

Loop of Henlé

Collecting duct

Blood to Renal Vein

Controlling Water Content of Blood

The amount of water reabsorbed by the kidneys, and so the concentration of urine, is controlled by the **anti-diuretic hormone** (**ADH**). ADH is produced by the pituitary gland. ADH directly affects the permeability of the renal tubules. It increases the permeability of the kidney tubules so more water is reabsorbed back into

the blood. This control mechanism is an example of **negative feedback**.

When water content of the body is low, ADH is released. This makes the tubules more permeable and more water is reabsorbed.

Dialysis

A **dialysis machine** can be used in patients with kidney failure to remove **urea** and maintain levels of sodium, water and glucose in the blood. Blood is taken from a vein and run into a dialysis machine. It comes into close contact with a partially permeable membrane, which separates the blood from the dialysis fluid. The waste diffuses from the blood into the dialysis fluid. The sodium and glucose are replaced in the blood.

Each dialysis session takes about three hours and must be carried out two or three times a week.

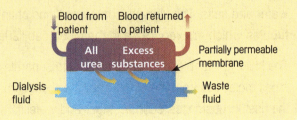

Blood from patient

Blood returned to patient

All urea

Excess substances

Partially permeable membrane

Dialysis fluid

Waste fluid

Sexual Reproduction

The diagrams show the key parts of the male and female reproductive systems.

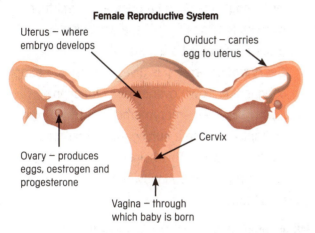

Female Reproductive System

Uterus – where embryo develops

Oviduct – carries egg to uterus

Cervix

Ovary – produces eggs, oestrogen and progesterone

Vagina – through which baby is born

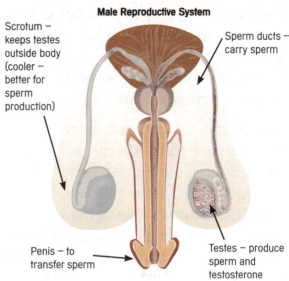

Male Reproductive System

Scrotum – keeps testes outside body (cooler – better for sperm production)

Sperm ducts – carry sperm

Penis – to transfer sperm

Testes – produce sperm and testosterone

These diagrams are not to scale.

The Menstrual Cycle

During the **menstrual cycle**, the uterus lining has different thicknesses. There are four stages:

1. The uterus lining breaks down (this is a period).
2. The uterus wall is repaired and gradually thickens.
3. An egg is released from one of the ovaries (**ovulation**).
4. The uterus lining stays thick in preparation for a **fertilised** egg. If no fertilised egg is detected, the cycle starts again.

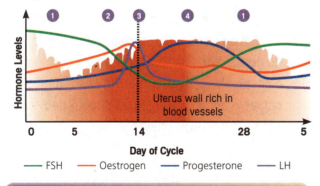

Hormone Levels

Uterus wall rich in blood vessels

Day of Cycle

0   5   14   28   5

— FSH   — Oestrogen   — Progesterone   — LH

FSH (follicle-stimulating hormone) is a **hormone** that stimulates the egg to ripen in the ovary. The ovary releases **oestrogen**, a hormone that stimulates the uterus lining to thicken, and stimulates the release of **LH** (luteinising hormone). LH is the hormone that controls **ovulation** about halfway through the menstrual cycle. After ovulation, **progesterone** is produced by the ovary to preserve the uterus lining. FSH and LH are released by the pituitary gland in the brain.

As oestrogen and progesterone levels fall towards the end of the cycle, **menstruation** occurs (i.e. the uterus lining breaks down).

HT **Negative Feedback**

The FSH stimulates the ovaries to secrete oestrogen. The oestrogen has a negative feedback effect, reducing FSH release.

Fertility in Humans

Fertility in humans can be controlled by the artificial use of sex hormones. Contraceptive pills and fertility drugs do this.

HT Hormonal contraceptives work by mimicking pregnancy and inhibiting FSH release.

B5 Life Goes On

Infertility Treatments

Fertilisation and pregnancy aren't guaranteed for everyone. Infertility may be caused by:

- blocked fallopian tubes or sperm ducts
- eggs not developing or being released from ovaries
- insufficient fertile sperm produced by testes.

But there are many methods that can help:

- **Fertility drugs** – **FSH** can be injected in women who don't produce enough FSH naturally. FSH stimulates eggs to ripen and be released.
- **Artificial insemination** – when the man's sperm count is low or the woman's oviducts are blocked, sperm is placed directly in the **uterus** and oviducts.
- *In vitro* **fertilisation** (**IVF**) – sperm and eggs are mixed together outside the body. The **embryos** that grow are transplanted into the uterus.
- **Egg donation** – if the woman doesn't produce fertile eggs, they can be donated by another woman, fertilised by IVF and transplanted. (Sperm can also be donated.)
- **Ovary transplant** – this gives a woman a supply of eggs if her own ovaries don't function.
- **Surrogacy** – an embryo produced by IVF can be implanted into a **surrogate mother** who carries the baby. This helps women who can't have a normal pregnancy or can't carry a baby to full-term.

When infertility treatments are successful, the result of a healthy baby for an infertile couple is wonderful.

Problems with Fertility Treatments

In **egg/sperm donation**, the embryo carries genes from only one parent and genes from a donor. **Surrogacy** can lead to emotional attachment, meaning the surrogate mother may find it hard to give the baby to its biological parents. **IVF** is expensive and doesn't have a high success rate. Twins or triplets are more likely to be produced as more than one embryo is implanted.

There is also the issue of what to do with leftover embryos that are no longer needed. Many people don't agree with disposing of human embryos. Some couples choose to give their unwanted embryos to another couple. Some may donate them to research, which raises more ethical and moral questions.

Foetal Screening

Ultrasound scans can reveal multiple pregnancies, developmental problems, or a baby's sex, early on in the pregnancy. **Amniocentesis** tests analyse cells from the foetus found in the amniotic fluid. A hypodermic needle is used to take a sample, which is checked for chromosome abnormalities, e.g. Down's Syndrome. Chromosome analysis can reveal serious conditions in the foetus.

Amniocentesis carries a risk of miscarriage (1 in 200) and, if an abnormality is detected, parents have to decide whether to continue the pregnancy. Some people think foetal screening offers the unacceptable option of ending an unborn baby's life, and that **termination** is unethical.

Quick Test

1. Name two female sex hormones.
2. What is the job of the testes?
3. Name three enzymes involved in digestion.
4. What is the job of the kidneys?

Key Words　　　　**Fertilisation • *In vitro* fertilisation • Ovary • Surrogacy**

Organ Donation

Due to disease or trauma, it's sometimes necessary to replace body parts with biological or mechanical parts.

Body parts from **human donors** can biologically replace the heart, lungs, kidney, blood, cornea and bone marrow.

Organs usually come from **dead donors**. A person's organs can be donated if they can't regain consciousness and can't breathe unaided. Some organs, e.g. a kidney, can come from a **living donor**. This is because the donor can live without the organ or tissue they have donated.

Donated organs must be:
- healthy
- the right size and age
- a good tissue match (otherwise the organ will be **rejected**).

Organs can only be donated if the donor is on the organ donor register and if their relatives have given their consent. There's always a shortage of donors.

Ethical issues

There are ethical issues with organ donation. Some people worry about signing up to be an organ donor – the effect it will have on their relatives and on their own body. Some people may not want to donate or receive organs due to religious or personal beliefs. There are many questions surrounding organ donation, e.g. should donors be allowed to receive money for donating organs? Can diseases be passed on to the recipient?

Problems with Organ Donation

If the donated organ isn't a good tissue match, the recipient's immune system will reject it. Organ recipients take **immunosuppressive drugs** for the rest of their lives to prevent rejection. But taking immunosuppressive drugs reduces their ability to fight other infections, making them more at risk of catching other diseases.

Organ Donation Issues

The UK has an '**opt-in**' donor system. Many people don't register as donors, so there's always a shortage of donors and a long wait for transplants. Many people think an '**opt-out**' system would be better. Sometimes the relatives of a person on the **National Register of Donors** don't agree to allow organ donation due to religious or cultural reasons.

In the UK, there's no payment for organ donation. It's been suggested that payment would increase availability. But this could encourage poor people to become donors in order to earn money.

Mechanical Replacements

Mechanical replacements include hip and knee joints, heart, lenses and kidneys. Implants must be:
- small and compact to fit inside the body
- made of materials that will not wear or cause allergic reactions, e.g. metals, plastics.

Some implants, such as pacemakers, need a reliable power supply. Batteries that can be recharged outside the body are now often used.

Some mechanical organ replacements, for example, heart-and-lung machines, kidney **dialysis machines** and mechanical ventilators work outside the body.

B5 Growth and Repair

Human Growth

There are five main stages in human **growth**:

1. Infancy (up to 2 years)
2. Childhood (2–11 years)
3. Puberty/adolescence (roughly 11–15 years)
4. Adulthood/maturity (roughly 15–65 years) – the longest stage
5. Old age (over 60–65 years)

The rate of growth is at a maximum when a baby is first born. Growth then slows down gradually during childhood. At puberty, there's another growth spurt. Growth stops in adulthood.

Measuring Human Growth

Human growth is measured in terms of gain in **height** or **mass**. A human foetus grows very quickly in the uterus. Different body parts develop at different rates. The brain and head develop quickly to coordinate the complex human structure and chemical activity.

A baby's head circumference, length and mass are measured regularly during the first few months. These measurements are plotted on average growth charts and compared with norms (average values for babies of their age) to indicate whether there are any growth problems. Average growth charts are simply a guide to show a comparison. Babies' growth can be above or below the average and still be totally healthy.

Example

The **mass** and **head circumference** of a baby were measured once a month for a year. The measurements are plotted on the graphs. By comparing the baby's measurements to the normal range, you can see that the baby's measurements were towards the lower end of healthy weight and head circumference, so no cause for concern. If the measurements were consistently above or below the healthy range, then the GP/health visitor may wish to investigate.

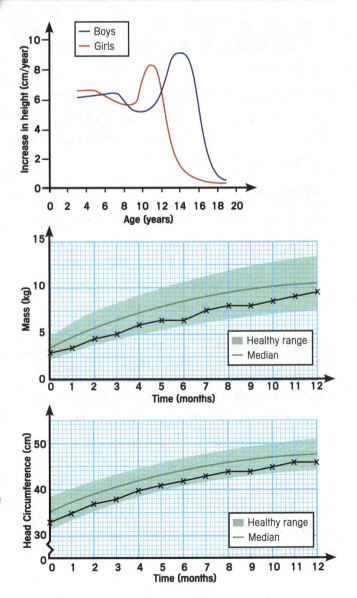

Factors Affecting Human Growth

Your eventual height and mass is determined by:

- inherited information in your **genes**
- your diet
- the amount of exercise you do
- the amount of growth **hormone** you produce
- how healthy you are
- any diseases/conditions you may have had
- hormones.

Diet is very important. A healthy diet contains protein for muscle growth, and calcium and vitamin D for bone growth.

Exercise is needed to encourage muscle growth, and to make bones dense and hard (strong).

Extremes of height are usually caused by genes or by an imbalance in the amount of growth hormone. For example:

- people who don't produce enough growth hormone aren't very tall and are called **dwarfs**
- people who produce too much growth hormone are very tall and are called **giants**.

HT Human growth hormone is produced by the pituitary gland in the brain, which stimulates the growth especially of long bones.

Life Expectancy

Life expectancy has greatly increased in recent years. This is due to:

- healthier diets and lifestyle

- modern treatments and cures for diseases
- better housing conditions, e.g. sewage disposal
- fewer **industrial diseases**, e.g. asbestosis.

HT Problems with Living Longer

Longer life expectancy brings its own problems:

- Elderly people can suffer from **degenerative diseases** such as **arthritis** and **cancer**.
- Elderly people might find it difficult to live independently in their own homes.
- The trend for small families means many elderly people will have no-one to look after them.
- Many pensioners live on a low income so it's difficult for them to maintain a healthy lifestyle.

All these problems reflect on society:

- Hospitals and care homes must cater for the short-term health needs of the elderly, but they also need to consider the residential needs of the increasing population of elderly patients.
- People of working age have to work longer and pay higher taxes to pay the pensions of the elderly population.

Quick Test

1. Give two reasons why life expectancy has increased.
2. What factors must be correct for a successful organ transplant?
3. What are the issues with foetal screening?

B5 Exam Practice Questions

1 The diagram shows the apparatus used in an experiment to mimic the workings of the small intestine. The distilled water was tested for starch and sugar at the beginning and end of the experiment. At the start of the experiment neither carbohydrate was present. At the end however, there was a positive test for sugar. Use your knowledge of absorption to explain these results.

[3]

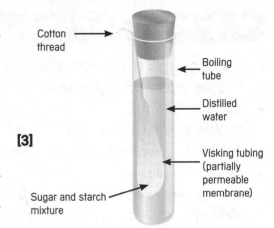

Cotton thread

Boiling tube

Distilled water

Visking tubing (partially permeable membrane)

Sugar and starch mixture

....

....

....

2 Noah has just returned from a skiing holiday, where he fell over and injured himself. Noah had to have an X-ray to see if he had broken any bones. This was his X-ray.

a) What is the name given to this type of fracture? .... **[1]**

b) Noah also complained that his right elbow was painful. **[1]**

    i) What type of joint is the elbow joint?

    ....

    ii) How are bones joined to other bones at joints? Put a ring around the correct answer in this list. **[1]**

    Cartilage   **Ligaments**   **Tendons**

3 a) Lee goes for a quick run and manages to run one mile in 7 minutes. When he finishes, he measures his pulse rate every minute for five minutes. His pulse rate returns to normal in five minutes.

Draw a graph to show Lee's pulse rate, starting at one minute. **[2]**

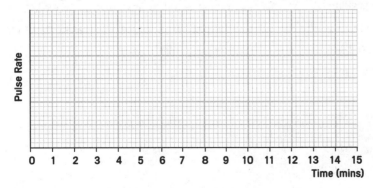

b) Explain why the pulse rate changes during exercise, in the way you have shown on the graph. **[2]**

....

4 Look at the diagram of the female reproductive system.

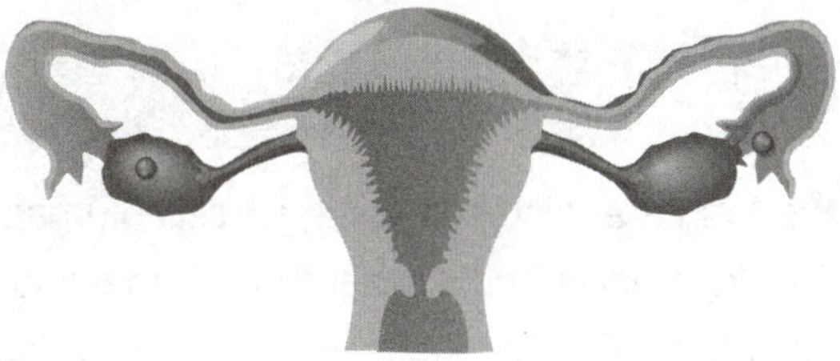

a) Which two hormones are produced in the ovaries? [2]

b) Name the hormone that stimulates the egg to ripen in the ovary. [1]

5 A baby was weighed every month for a year after it was born. The baby's mass every month was recorded on the graph opposite.

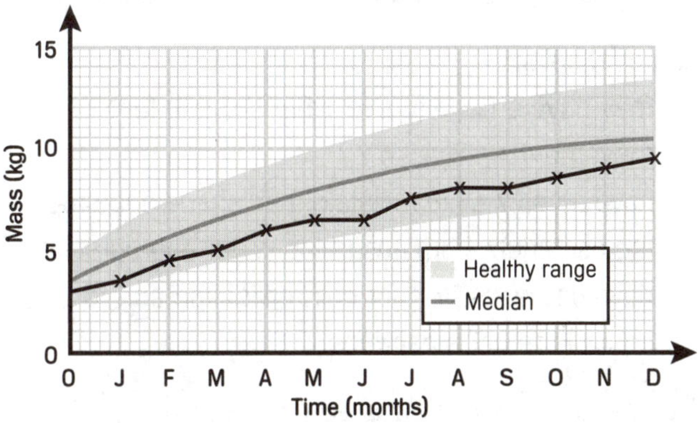

a) Describe the overall change in the baby's mass. Also discuss the mass in relation to the healthy range. [3]

b) By how much did the baby's mass increase between March and July? [1]

6 Scientists have been studying the body of an Egyptian king who died thousands of years ago. Statues of the king show that he had very long arms. The scientists have taken X-rays of the king's bones to see if he was still growing at the time of his death, and so work out his age.

a) What factors may affect a person's growth? [3]

b) Other statues showed that other Egyptians around the same time also had long arms. Suggest reasons why. [2]

HT 7 John has been in a car accident and requires a blood transfusion. Blood tests reveal that his blood type is O positive. Explain, using ideas about antigens and antibodies, why the doctors cannot give John blood which is A positive. [3]

B6 Understanding Microbes

Bacterial Cells

Bacteria are microscopic single-celled organisms. They're smaller and simpler than animal and plant cells. The largest bacteria are only a few microns (i.e. thousandths of a millimetre) long.

Bacterial cells are simpler than plant and animal cells: bacterial cells don't have a 'true' nucleus, mitochondria, chloroplasts or a vacuole.

Describing Bacterial Cells

Bacterial cells:

- may have a **flagellum** (a whip-like tail) for movement
- have a **cell wall** to maintain their shape and stop the bacterium from absorbing water and bursting
- have **bacterial DNA** for cell replication and to control the cell's activities.

A bacterial cell can be classified by its shape:

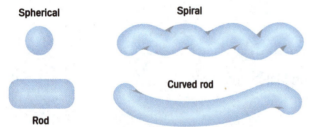

Spherical

Spiral

Curved rod

Rod

E. coli – An Example of a Flagellate Bacillus

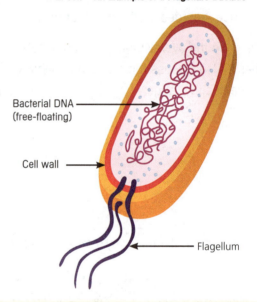

Bacterial DNA (free-floating)

Cell wall

Flagellum

HT Bacterial Food Sources

Bacteria get their food from different sources. Some bacteria feed on organic nutrients.

Some bacteria make their own food in a similar way to plants. Because bacteria can use so many different sources of nutrients and energy, they're able to survive in a variety of habitats, for example:

- hot springs
- acid peat bogs
- inside humans.

Bacterial Reproduction

Bacteria **reproduce asexually** by splitting in two. This is called **binary fission**.

Bacteria reproduce rapidly in the right conditions. They can be grown commercially on a large scale in tanks called **fermenters**.

HT **Bacteria** grow and reproduce quickly. This means:

- diseases spread quickly as conditions inside the human body are ideal for bacterial growth (warm, moist, food available)
- food can become contaminated by bacteria and the toxic waste produced by bacteria as they feed. Food can spoil very quickly.

Key Words   Bacteria • Flagellum • DNA • Fermenter

Viruses

Viruses are not living cells. They can only reproduce in other living cells. They attack specific cells and can infect plant, bacterial or animal cells. They are much smaller than bacteria or fungi.

Strand of genetic material

Protein coat

HT To invade a living cell:
1. The virus attaches to a host cell and injects its genetic material into the cell.
2. It uses the cell to make components for a new virus.
3. The host cell splits open to release the virus.

Yeast

Yeast is a single-celled **fungus**. Yeast cells reproduce asexually by **budding**.

Yeast cells reproduce very quickly under the right conditions. They need:

- lots of sugar
- optimum temperature and pH
- the removal of waste products, such as **alcohol**, which poison the yeast.

The chromosomes are copied and a new nucleus is made. The new cell 'buds' off the parent. This is known as 'budding'.

HT **Temperature and Yeast Growth**

The growth rate of yeast doubles with every 10°C rise in temperature. So, increasing the temperature increases the rate of **growth**. But, above 40°C, the yeast enzymes are **denatured**, which causes the growth rate to slow down.

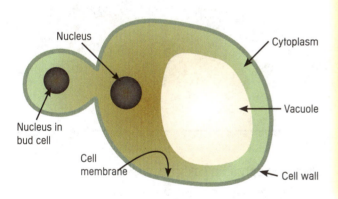

Nucleus

Cytoplasm

Vacuole

Nucleus in bud cell

Cell membrane

Cell wall

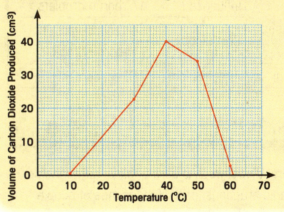

Aseptic Techniques

Aseptic technique is the process of growing and transferring bacteria without contaminating the sample by touching or breathing on it, and without any loss of microbes to the surroundings.

Sterile agar plates are prepared with nutrient agar containing the food and water microbes need to grow. Use a sterile swab to wipe across the area you wish to test for microbes. Quickly lift just a corner of the agar plate (just enough to wipe the swab across the

surface of the agar). Swiftly replace the lid and seal it down. Incubate in a warm place. After 24 hours, colonies of bacteria will be visible. Do not re-open.

HT It's important to safely handle bacteria by using aseptic technique. This ensures that no unexpected harmful bacteria are grown in large amounts which could make people ill. It safeguards people from being exposed to pathogenic microbes.

B6 Harmful Microorganisms

Pathogens

Pathogens are **microorganisms** that cause disease. Some bacteria are pathogens. **Viruses** and **fungi** can also be pathogens.

Pathogens reproduce very quickly once inside the body. This is the disease's incubation period and initially there might not be any symptoms. As they multiply, pathogens produce **toxins**, which start to give the symptoms of the disease, such as fever.

Pathogens can enter your body in different ways:

- Airborne microorganisms enter through your **nose**.
- Microorganisms in contaminated food and water enter through your **mouth**.
- Microorganisms can be injected through the skin, e.g. **insect bites**, **infected needles** or **wounds**.
- Microorganisms can be passed on through the reproductive organs **during sex**.

Diseases

Different pathogens cause different diseases.

Pathogen	Illness Caused	How it's Transmitted
Bacteria	Cholera	Contaminated water
	Food poisoning	Contaminated food
Viruses	Influenza	Airborne droplets
	Chickenpox	Direct contact or airborne droplets
Fungi	Athlete's foot	Direct contact

Natural Disasters

Natural disasters, like earthquakes, hurricanes or volcanic eruptions, can kill thousands of people.

Many die in the aftermath of a natural disaster due to the rapid spread of diseases such as cholera and food poisoning.

Diseases spread quickly because:

- sewage systems and water supplies can be damaged so drinking water gets contaminated
- electrical supplies can be damaged so fridges and freezers stop working and food goes off
- the energy supply is disrupted, making it difficult to cook food properly
- hospitals and medical supplies get destroyed
- roads may be damaged, making it hard to reach sick or injured people.

The Germ Theory of Disease

In the 1860s, **Louis Pasteur** showed that microorganisms in the air were the cause of food decay (not just the air itself, as people had previously thought).

This led to the **germ theory of disease** which explained that microorganisms, passed from one person to another, caused many diseases.

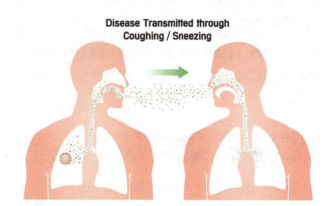

Disease Transmitted through Coughing / Sneezing

The Development of Antiseptics

In 1865, **Lister**, a surgeon, noticed that wounds often became infected after operations.

He realised that spraying wounds with **carbolic acid** prevented wound infection.

Carbolic acid is an **antiseptic** and kills bacteria.

Antiseptics are used today to kill bacteria in wounds on the skin, so preventing the spread of disease.

The Discovery of Penicillin

In 1928, **Fleming** accidentally discovered **penicillin**, an **antibiotic**.

When some of his bacterial culture plates got contaminated with penicillium mould, he noticed that the mould killed the surrounding bacteria.

He used the mould to make the first antibiotic to treat bacterial infections.

Harmful bacteria can be controlled by using antibiotics, but viruses are unaffected by antibiotics. Due to the overuse of antibiotics, some bacteria have developed resistance to them through natural selection.

Some strains of bacteria are developing resistance to antibiotics through **natural selection**.

One bacterium may survive the antibiotic treatment due to a genetic change. This bacterium can then rapidly multiply, producing millions of resistant bacterial cells leading to an infection that is resistant to antibiotic treatment. This has become a huge problem recently.

HT To reduce the appearance of bacteria which are resistant to antibiotics, doctors now only prescribe antibiotics where really necessary and patients should always complete the treatment.

Quick Test

1. Describe the structure of a virus.
2. List the main shapes of bacteria.
3. How can microbes enter the body?
4. Which scientist did pioneering work on developing antiseptics?

Key Words   Antiseptic • Penicillin • Antibiotics

B6 Useful Microorganisms

Useful Bacteria

Not all bacteria are harmful.

We use bacteria to make a range of useful products including compost and silage (winter feed for cattle), vinegar, cheese and yoghurt.

Making Yoghurt

Yoghurt is made in large steel **fermenters**:

1. The equipment is sterilised using steam to kill any **pathogens**.
2. Raw milk is heated to 80°C to kill bacteria, and then quickly cooled. This is **pasteurisation**.
3. A live bacterial culture is added to the warm milk. The mixture is **incubated** for several hours.
4. The bacteria reproduce and feed on the **lactose** sugar in the milk, producing **lactic acid**, which gives a sharp taste to the yoghurt and thickens and preserves it.
5. The manufacturer **samples** the yoghurt for consistency and flavour.
6. Flavours and colours might be added before packaging.

HT The bacteria *Lactobacillus* feed on the lactose sugar in the milk, breaking it down to produce lactic acid, which gives the yoghurt its taste and texture.

Fermentation

Fermentation is **anaerobic respiration** in yeast. It produces alcohol and is used to make alcoholic drinks.

Sugars are broken down by yeast in the absence of oxygen to produce the alcohol.

Different fruits and seeds are used to provide the **yeast** with sugars and give the drinks flavour.

Carbon dioxide is also produced during fermentation:

glucose (sugar)	$\rightarrow$	ethanol (alcohol)	+	carbon dioxide
HT $C_6H_{12}O_6$	$\rightarrow$	$2C_2H_5OH$	+	$2CO_2$

Fermentation (Cont.)

Yeast cells feed on **sugars**. They can respire with oxygen (**aerobic respiration**) or without oxygen (**anaerobic respiration**) to release energy from sugar.

Brewers obviously want yeast to carry out anaerobic respiration as alcohol is a by-product.

Brewing Beer

1. Extracting sugar – barley seeds are mixed with water and allowed to sprout, turning the starch in the seeds into sugars.
2. Hops are added to give flavour to beer.
3. Yeast is added to ferment the sugars into alcohol. The mixture is kept warm so the yeast **reproduces** and **respires**.
4. The tank is sealed so the yeast can respire **anaerobically** producing alcohol. This also stops unwanted microorganisms spoiling the beer.
5. A chemical is added to make the yeast settle, leaving a clear liquid. This is called **clarifying** or **clearing**.
6. The beer is **pasteurised** to kill harmful microorganisms.
7. The beer is bottled or put in sealed casks (casking or bottling).

Yeast must be filtered out (or killed by heat treatment) if the beer's going to be bottled. Otherwise, it would continue to respire, producing carbon dioxide which would make the bottles explode.

Beer is pasteurised by heating to 72°C for 15 seconds, then cooling quickly. This kills harmful microorganisms but doesn't affect the taste much. This needs to be done to bottled beers to prevent spoilage by microbes.

Distilling Spirits

Distillation of alcoholic drinks makes the alcohol more concentrated and is used to produce spirits. Because it produces very strong alcoholic drinks, distillation can only be done on licensed premises; it is a commercial process.

1. The liquid is heated to evaporate the alcohol.
2. The concentrated alcohol is trapped and cooled (condensed) back into a liquid.

The amount of alcohol in brewed drinks is limited because the yeast cells are killed by the alcohol they produce.

Some strains of yeast can tolerate higher concentrations of alcohol so they can be used to brew strong beers.

Quick Test

1. Suggest some useful ways in which bacteria are used.
2. What process is used to increase the alcoholic content of drinks?
3. HT Is fermentation an aerobic or anaerobic process?
4. HT What do *Lactobacillus* bacteria do in the yoghurt making process?

B6 Biofuels

Biofuels

Plants grow new plant tissues by using some of the glucose from **photosynthesis** to produce starch and cellulose. This new plant material is **biomass**.

Biomass can be **burned** to release energy to be used as a **fuel**. Some examples of biomass fuels are:

- **fast-growing trees**, e.g. pine burned to release energy

- **manure** or **other waste** – broken down by **bacteria** or **yeast** in a **fermenter** to release methane (**biogas**) which can be used to power electricity generators
- **sugar cane** – broken down by yeast in a fermenter to produce alcohol.

Biogas

When these bacteria feed on dead plant and animal material, they produce waste gases called **biogas**. Biogas contains:

- mainly methane
- some carbon dioxide
- traces of hydrogen, nitrogen and hydrogen sulfide.

HT Biogas is a cleaner fuel than petrol or diesel, but it doesn't produce as much energy as natural gas.

- Biogas that contains more than 50% methane burns easily and makes a good fuel.
- Biogas that contains less than 10% methane is explosive.

Biogas Digesters

Biogas (mainly methane) can be made on a large scale using a **continuous flow method** in a **digester**. Organic material is added daily and the biogas is siphoned off and stored. The remaining solid sludge is used as **fertiliser**. The production of biogas is affected by temperature. At low temperatures, little biogas is produced. Above 45°C, no biogas is released.

Biogas digesters are useful in remote areas that don't have access to mains electricity. They can produce biogas from human sewage, which also solves the problem of safe sewage disposal. Biogas can be:

- burned to generate electricity, and to produce hot water and steam for central heating
- used as a fuel for buses and cars.

The rotting of organic material such as dead plants and animal waste occurs mainly in marshes, septic tanks and animal digestive systems. It produces a mixture of gases including methane, thanks to the action of bacteria.

Methane is given off in landfill sites as the microbes feed on the rubbish. This is dangerous as it's explosive. The site may not be safe to use for years.

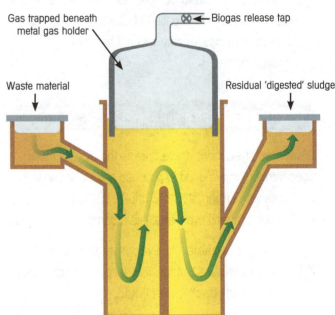

A Biogas Digester

Gas trapped beneath metal gas holder

Biogas release tap

Waste material

Residual 'digested' sludge

HT At low temperatures, the bacteria reproduce and respire slowly so little biogas is produced. At above 45°C, enzymes in the bacteria are **denatured** and the bacteria are killed. This is why biogas production is so dependent on temperature.

Photosynthesis • Biomass • Biogas • Fertiliser

Biofuel

Biofuels, such as biogas, are a good alternative to fossil fuels, because burning biofuels produces:

- no increase in greenhouse gas levels
- no soot (particulates).

HT Burning biofuels doesn't cause an overall increase in greenhouse gas levels if:

- they are burned at the same rate as the biomass is being produced
- areas of land are not cleared of other vegetation in order to grow crops for biofuels.

In some areas, the use of large areas of land to produce biofuels is resulting in habitat loss and the potential extinction of species.

Alcohol, made from yeast, can also be used as a clean biofuel. Alcohol doesn't contain as much energy as petrol so it's mixed with petrol or diesel to make **gasohol**, which is used to run cars in countries like Brazil.

HT In countries like Brazil, gasohol is more economically viable because they have little or no oil reserves from which to produce fuel to run cars.

They do, however, have plenty sugar cane and so they ferment this to produce alcohol which is used to make gasohol.

Quick Test

1. Give two examples of fuels from biomass.
2. How can biogas be produced on a large scale?
3. What are the advantages of using biofuels?
4. What is the name of the biofuel used in Brazil to power cars?

B6 Life in Soil

Soil

Soil is a mixture of:
- different sized mineral particles
- **humus** (dead animal and plant material)
- water
- living organisms (e.g. microscopic protozoans, nematode worms, earthworms, insects, slugs, snails, bacteria)
- air (oxygen).

Living organisms need oxygen so they can respire, and water to stay alive. Soil provides both of these.

Plants need soil to grow. Soil provides them with:
- a source of minerals (e.g. nitrates, phosphates)
- water (for **photosynthesis** and **transpiration**)
- anchorage for roots (to hold the plant upright).

There are different types of soil, e.g. sandy, loam, clay. Sandy soil has larger mineral particles than clay soil. Loam is a soil that contains a mixture of clay and sand. If the dead material in soil is largely decomposed it is called **humus**.

HT When there's too much water in the soil, it leads to **waterlogging**: the water fills all the air spaces and excludes oxygen. Pushing holes into the soil aerates it, allowing oxygen to penetrate into it, and helping to drain the excess water.

Some soils are naturally **acidic**. This causes problems for organisms that can't survive in acidic conditions. It also means plants can't absorb minerals easily. So farmers and gardeners add **lime** to acidic soil to neutralise it. Mixing up the soil layers to distribute the lime helps neutralise the acid soil.

Humus

Humus is often described as the 'life force' of the soil. It helps soil to retain moisture and oxygen, which life in the soil depends on.

As it decomposes, important minerals are released for plant growth.

As humus particle size is quite big it increases the air spaces in soil and, so, the air content.

Humus • Photosynthesis • Transpiration

Soil Experiments

Different soils can be compared in terms of their water, air and humus content.

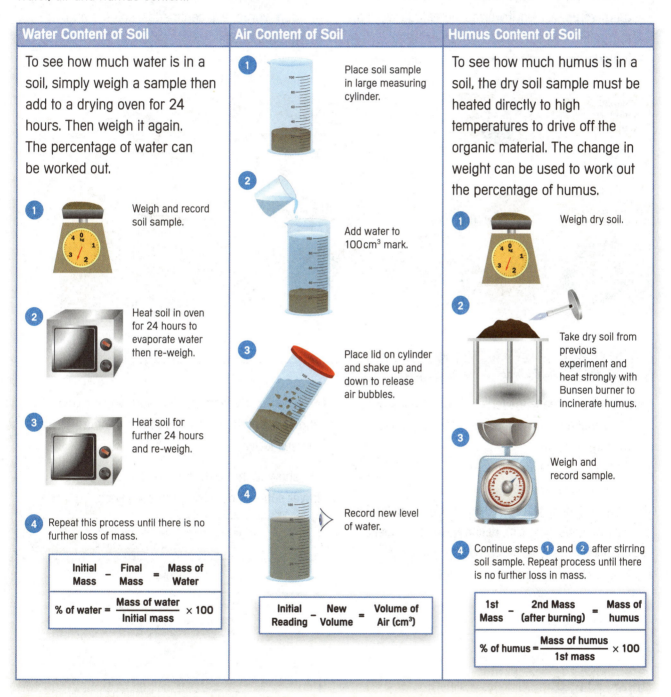

Water Content of Soil	Air Content of Soil	Humus Content of Soil

Water Content of Soil

To see how much water is in a soil, simply weigh a sample then add to a drying oven for 24 hours. Then weigh it again. The percentage of water can be worked out.

1. Weigh and record soil sample.

2. Heat soil in oven for 24 hours to evaporate water then re-weigh.

3. Heat soil for further 24 hours and re-weigh.

4. Repeat this process until there is no further loss of mass.

$$\text{Initial Mass} - \text{Final Mass} = \text{Mass of Water}$$

$$\% \text{ of water} = \frac{\text{Mass of water}}{\text{Initial mass}} \times 100$$

Air Content of Soil

1. Place soil sample in large measuring cylinder.

2. Add water to 100 cm^3 mark.

3. Place lid on cylinder and shake up and down to release air bubbles.

4. Record new level of water.

$$\text{Initial Reading} - \text{New Volume} = \text{Volume of Air (cm}^3\text{)}$$

Humus Content of Soil

To see how much humus is in a soil, the dry soil sample must be heated directly to high temperatures to drive off the organic material. The change in weight can be used to work out the percentage of humus.

1. Weigh dry soil.

2. Take dry soil from previous experiment and heat strongly with Bunsen burner to incinerate humus.

3. Weigh and record sample.

4. Continue steps 1 and 2 after stirring soil sample. Repeat process until there is no further loss in mass.

$$\text{1st Mass} - \text{2nd Mass (after burning)} = \text{Mass of humus}$$

$$\% \text{ of humus} = \frac{\text{Mass of humus}}{\text{1st mass}} \times 100$$

HT When a dry soil is heated to high temperatures, the humus, which is made of carbon compounds, is converted to carbon dioxide and water. These are given off as gases so the sample weight goes down.

The size and number of pores in the soil determine the air content. When it rains, the water fills the pores, driving out the air.

B6 Life in Soil

Food Webs in Soil

Complex food webs exist in soil. Soil contains:

- **herbivores**, e.g. slugs, snails, wire worms
- **detritivores**, e.g. earthworms, nematode worms, millipedes and springtails, which eat dead material and break it down into humus
- **decomposers**, e.g. fungi, and bacteria which break down the humus
- **carnivores**, e.g. centipedes, spiders and ground beetles.

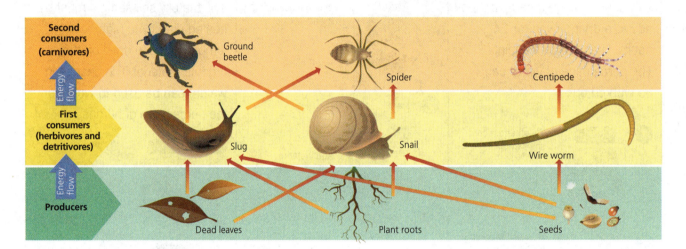

Second consumers (carnivores) — Ground beetle, Spider, Centipede

Energy flow

First consumers (herbivores and detritivores) — Slug, Snail, Wire worm

Energy flow

Producers — Dead leaves, Plant roots, Seeds

Earthworms

Earthworms increase the fertility and drainage of soil:

- They make burrows through the soil layers, mixing them up.
- They create drainage and air channels (aeration) with their burrows.
- They drag dead leaves and other organic matter into their burrows, where it's **decomposed** by bacteria and fungi. This releases **nutrients** into the soil.
- They help to **neutralise** acidic soil.

HT Charles Darwin studied earthworms and showed that they were very important in keeping the soil fertile.

He showed that they increased the fertility of the lower sub-soil by mixing the soil layers.

> An organic humus layer is formed on top of the soil as a result of decomposition.

> Nutrients (minerals) are released from the decomposing material.

> The nutrients are taken down into the deeper soil layers by earthworms. This prevents the nutrients from being washed away and it also aerates the soil and breaks it up.

Recycling is important so that the mineral elements trapped in the bodies of dead organisms can be made available to living organisms.

Quick Test

1. Describe the main components in soil.
2. What does soil do for plants?
3. Name some herbivores in soil.
4. How can you improve soil?

Key Words   Herbivore • Detritivore • Decomposers • Carnivore

Microscopic Life in Water B6

Life in Water

A wide variety of microorganisms live in water.

Advantages of Living in Water	Disadvantages of Living in Water
• No problem of water shortage or dehydration. • Less variation in temperature. • Water gives more support so organisms grow bigger without huge increases in skeleton size. • Waste is easily disposed of.	• Water is dense so it resists movement. • It might be difficult to control the absorption or release of water from living cells.

Marine Food Webs

Plankton are microscopic plants and animals. **Phytoplankton** (microscopic plants) and **zooplankton** (microscopic animals) live in water. Plankton have limited movement and rely on water currents.

Phytoplankton are the **producers** in aquatic food chains and food webs.

Phytoplankton make sugars by **photosynthesis**. Their growth is affected by temperature, light intensity and availability of minerals like nitrates and phosphates.

In summer, when conditions are good (light, warm, lots of minerals), the plankton grow quickly. In winter (less light, colder, fewer minerals), their growth slows down.

Light intensity and temperature vary at different depths.

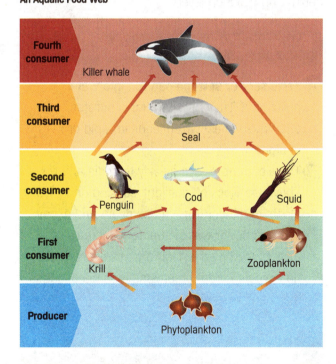

An Aquatic Food Web

HT Grazing food webs are most common in the oceans.

In the ocean depths many organisms rely on **marine snow**. Marine snow is the continuous shower of organic detritus falling from the upper layers of the ocean. It's made mainly of dead and dying plants and animals (e.g. plankton) and faecal material. Most marine snow is consumed by microbes and zooplankton and filter feeding animals. As sunlight can't reach deep sea ecosystems, these organisms rely heavily on marine snow.

Deep in the ocean some bacteria act as producers, making their own food like plants do. They have no light to do this but instead use other chemicals to make glucose. Many food chains in the deep dark ocean rely on these bacteria.

B6 Microscopic Life in Water

Water Pollution

Animals, plants and microorganisms are all affected by water **pollution** from:

- sewage
- oil
- PCBs (chemicals used in electrical devices)
- **fertilisers**
- pesticides
- detergents.

Aquatic microorganisms are very sensitive to pollution and pH changes caused by **acid rain**. The variety and number of aquatic microorganisms will depend on pollution levels.

Eutrophication

1. **Fertilisers** or **sewage** can run into water, polluting it. They provide a lot of nitrates and phosphates, which leads to rapid growth of **algae**.
2. The algae reproduce quickly then die and rot. They also block off sunlight, causing underwater plants to die and rot – mass death and decay.
3. The number of **aerobic bacteria** increase and, as they feed on the dead organisms, they use up oxygen. Larger organisms then die because they can't **respire**.

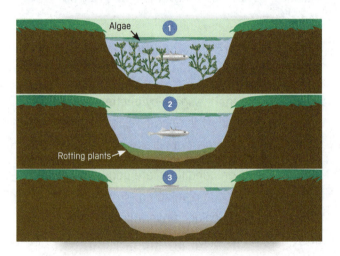

Algae ①

Rotting plants ②

③

HT Bioaccumulation

Small amounts of toxic chemicals, such as PCBs and DDT, enter the food chain through **plankton**:

- **PCBs** are chemicals used to insulate electrical equipment.
- **DDT** is a powerful persistent insecticide.

If animals eat these chemicals, they can't break them down so they're stored in fat in the body.

Small amounts don't cause any harm, but at each trophic feeding level the chemicals accumulate in the tissues of the animals.

For example, if a whale eats penguins and seals that have eaten contaminated fish, the accumulative effect of the **toxins** can be enough to kill it.

Animals at the top of food chains like whales get a huge dose of these chemicals so they may die.

Pollution • Fertiliser • Respiration

Biological Indicators

Some animal species are very good **indicators** of water's cleanliness. They act as biological indicators for pH and oxygen levels.

For example, some insect larvae like mayfly or stonefly are sensitive to changes in oxygen and can only survive in clean, oxygenated water. Other insect larvae, like bloodworms and rat-tailed maggots, have special adaptations to survive in **polluted**, deoxygenated water.

Counting the total number of indicator organisms and the number of different species (the **biodiversity**) can show how polluted the water is.

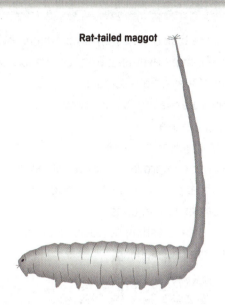

Rat-tailed maggot

HT Problems of Living in Water

Some microscopic organisms, such as amoeba, find it difficult to balance water. This is due to **osmosis**.

An amoeba is a single-celled organism that lives in freshwater. The water is more dilute than the amoeba's **cytoplasm** so water constantly **diffuses** into the cell by osmosis. The amoeba doesn't have a cell wall to prevent it bursting, so it has to use **active transport** to pump the water into **small vacuoles**. These small vacuoles join into one **contractile vacuole** which empties the water out of the cell.

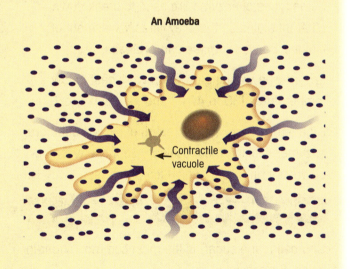

An Amoeba

Contractile vacuole

Quick Test

1. What is phytoplankton?
2. Name some pollutants of water.
3. What is the root cause of eutrophication?
4. HT DDT is a persistent pesticide. What organisms are most at risk from it and why?

B6 Enzymes in Action

Using Enzymes

Enzymes are biological **catalysts** produced by living cells. They can be extracted from cells and used in a number of ways. For example:

- to separate the curds and whey when making cheese
- to extract juice from fruit
- to alter and improve the flavour of foods
- in medical products, such as **reagent sticks** that test for **glucose** in urine
- in biological washing powders to break down food stains on clothing.

HT In areas with very acidic or very alkaline tap water, the enzymes don't work so well: the extreme pH changes the enzymes' shape, so they can't function. They are **denatured**.

Biological Washing Powders

Biological washing powders contain enzymes. Food, blood and grass stains on clothes are made from large insoluble molecules that are hard to wash away.

Three types of enzyme are used to break down different stains so that they'll easily wash out of clothes: **amylase**, **lipase** and **protease**.

Enzymes in washing powders work best at low temperatures (30 to 40°C) and neutral pH (pH 7).

High temperature and extremes of pH will denature enzymes making them useless. So these washing powders don't work at high temperatures.

HT The soluble products of digestion are easily washed out of clothes.

Enzyme	Insoluble Stain	Soluble Product
Amylase	Carbohydrate, e.g. starch	**HT** Sugars
Lipase	Fat	**HT** Fatty acids, glycerol
Protease	Protein	**HT** Amino acids

Sweetening Food

Sucrose (cane sugar) is the most common sugar in foods. Sucrose:

- is made up of two smaller sugars
- can be broken down using the **sucrase** (or **invertase**) enzyme.

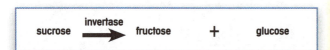

sucrose $\xrightarrow{\text{invertase}}$ fructose + glucose

The products are much sweeter than sucrose. They're useful in the food industry for flavouring desserts and sweets without adding much sugar.

HT Foods are sweetened using invertase by converting sucrose into fructose and glucose. These much sweeter products are used to sweeten diet food/low calorie food so less sugar is needed, meaning fewer calories are in the food.

Nutrition Information		
Typical Values	Flora light Per 100g	Flora light Per 10g
Energy	1459kJ/354kcal	146kj/35kcal
Carbohydrate	2.8g	0.3g
- of which Sugars	trace	trace
Fat	38.0g	3.8g
- of which saturates	9.3g	0.9g
- monounsaturates	9.3g	0.9g
- polyunsaturates	19.0g	1.9g
Sodium	0.5g	0.1g
Salt (based on sodium)	1.3g	0.1g

HT Lactose-free Milk

Some adults are **lactose intolerant**. This means they don't make the enzyme **lactase**, so they can't break down the lactose sugar in milk. As a result, lactose travels through their digestive system to the large intestine, where bacteria ferment the sugar, producing diarrhoea and gas.

Enzymes can be used to make lactose-free milk. Immobilised lactase enzyme can be added to the milk to break down lactose sugar into smaller sugars – **glucose** and **galactose** – which can easily be absorbed.

Adult cats can't digest cows' milk because they don't produce lactase, so they suffer from the same problems. This is why cat food manufacturers now make lactose-free cat milk.

Immobilised Enzymes

Extracting and purifying enzymes is an expensive business. So it's useful to be able to reclaim the enzymes after the reaction, to reuse them.

This is also important in food preparation because the enzymes mustn't contaminate the final food products.

Enzymes can be immobilised by:
- making them into alginate jelly beads (gel beads)
- putting them on reagent sticks.

They can then be easily separated from the reaction mixture. The mixture is not contaminated with enzymes. Immobilising enzymes in these ways is also useful because it means they can be used in **continuous flow processing**.

To make gel beads, the enzymes are mixed with alginate and the mixture is dropped into calcium chloride solution.

Testing for Sugar

People who have **diabetes** have to test their urine or blood for sugar every day to check blood glucose levels and to ensure they inject the right amount of **insulin**.

The **Benedict's test** can be used to test for sugar, but a large sample of blood or urine is needed. The sample is heated with Benedict's reagent. If the blue reagent turns red, then sugar is present.

Reagent sticks make it easy to test blood sugar. Immobilised enzymes are often incorporated onto reagent sticks e.g. the stick is dipped in urine or blood and changes colour according to the glucose level.

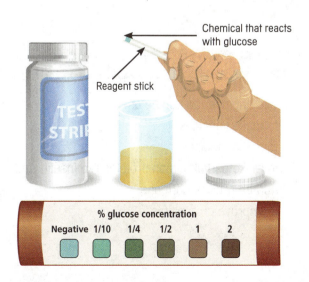

Chemical that reacts with glucose

Reagent stick

% glucose concentration

Negative 1/10 1/4 1/2 1 2

Genetic Engineering

All living organisms use the same basic genetic code (DNA), so genes can be transferred from one organism to another altering the genetic code.

Genes from one organism can work in another. This is **genetic engineering**.

Section of DNA

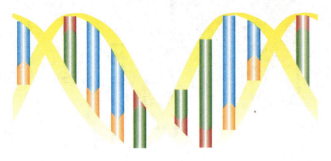

The genetic code is universal; the DNA structure for all organisms is the same.

Because of this, genes from one organism can work in another organism, making genetic engineering possible.

Genetic engineering can be used to change the characteristics of bacteria, plants or animals. An organism that has new genes inserted into it is called a **transgenic organism**.

1. The desirable gene in one organism is identified.
2. The gene is removed from the DNA.
3. The DNA of another organism is cut open and the new gene is inserted.
4. The new gene works in the transgenic organism.
5. The transgenic organism is **cloned** to produce identical copies.

HT Different enzymes are used in genetic engineering:

- **Restriction enzymes** are used to cut open DNA leaving 'sticky ends'.
- **Ligase enzymes** are used to rejoin DNA strands. The 'sticky ends' rejoin the DNA strands.

Scientists use a technique called **assaying** to identify transgenic organisms because not all the bacteria will take up the new genes. When the new gene is inserted, a 'marker gene', for example, a gene that codes for **antibiotic resistance**, is also inserted.

The bacteria are then grown on an agar plate that contains the antibiotic. The transgenic bacteria can be identified because they survive and grow.

Uses of Genetic Engineering

Genetic engineering can be used:
- to make vaccines
- to make medicines
- to make useful human proteins like insulin and human growth hormone
- to improve crop plants.

Producing Human Insulin

(HT) The loop of bacterial DNA is known as a **plasmid**. Plasmids are found in the cytoplasm of the bacterial cells.

Human **insulin** is produced using the following method:

1. The human gene for insulin production is identified. It's removed using a special **enzyme** which cuts through the **DNA** in precise places.
2. The enzyme is then used to cut open a loop of bacterial DNA in the cytoplasm.
3. Enzymes are used to insert the section of human insulin gene into the loop.

4. The loop is reinserted into a bacterium which starts to divide rapidly. As it divides, it replicates the loop, and makes insulin.
5. The transgenic bacteria are cultured by cloning in large **fermenters**. Each bacterium carries instructions to make insulin. When the bacteria make the protein, commercial (large) quantities of insulin can be harvested. Because these loops can be taken up by bacteria, they can be used as vectors in genetic engineering.

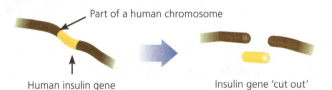
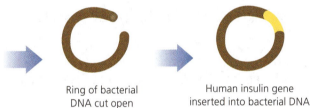

Part of a human chromosome

Human insulin gene

Insulin gene 'cut out'

Ring of bacterial DNA cut open

Human insulin gene inserted into bacterial DNA

DNA Fingerprinting

Each person's DNA is **unique**, so it can be used for **identification** in a technique called **DNA fingerprinting**. For example, blood found at a crime scene can be compared with samples of suspects' DNA.

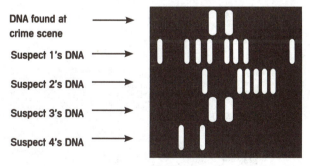

DNA found at crime scene

Suspect 1's DNA

Suspect 2's DNA

Suspect 3's DNA

Suspect 4's DNA

You can see that the unique DNA fingerprint from the blood sample found at the crime scene matches exactly with the DNA fingerprint of Suspect 3.

Keeping a central database for genetic fingerprints would be very helpful to crime prevention agencies like the Police. It could be used to help solve crimes. But many people don't like this idea, and think DNA is private.

(HT) To make a DNA fingerprint, a sample of DNA is needed. DNA fingerprinting is carried out in four stages:

1. **Extraction** – DNA is extracted from blood, hair follicles or semen.
2. **Fragmentation** – the DNA is cut into fragments using **restriction** enzymes.
3. **Separation** – the DNA sections are separated using a technique called **electrophoresis**.
4. **Visualising pattern** – the DNA fingerprint is analysed by comparing it with a reference sample, e.g. blood taken from the crime scene.

Quick Test

1. How can enzymes be immobilised?
2. What is genetic engineering?
3. Explain why biological washing powders will not work at high temperatures.

1 Adrian has an intolerance to milk. He has to drink lactose-free milk. He is keen to find out how it is made.

a) Why is it best to use immobilised enzymes to break down lactose in milk? **[1]**

b) Explain why people with diabetes might use immobilised enzymes. **[1]**

2 After the year 11 prom Sabrina finds some food stains on her dress. Her mum suggests that she should use a biological washing powder to remove the stains. Sabrina reads the following contents on the packet of biological washing powder:

Sodium carbonate to soften water 15%   Soap 45%
Perfume 10%   Protease enzymes 5%
Antifoam agent 5%   Brightening compounds 10%
Oxidising agents 10%

a) The concentration of enzymes is very low. Why? **[1]**

b) Sabrina washes her dress at 60°C. Explain whether you think she was correct to do this. **[1]**

c) i) There are three different stains on Sabrina's dress: egg, butter and ketchup. Which one will be removed most easily by the washing powder? **[1]**

ii) Explain your answer. **[3]**

3 Look at this marine food web.

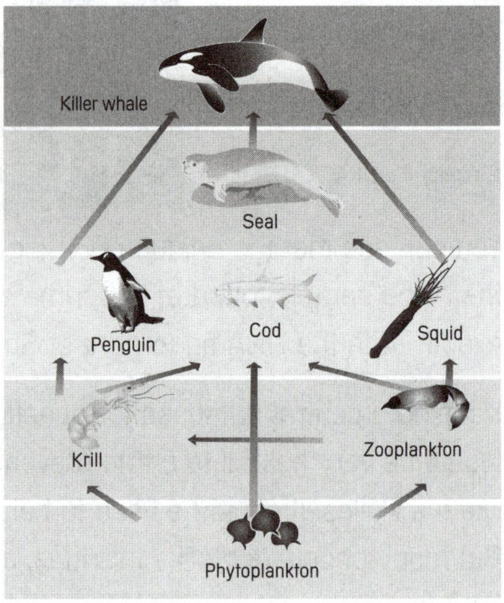

a) What are the secondary consumers in this food web? **[1]**

b) i) What are phytoplankton? **[1]**

ii) List the factors that affect the growth of phytoplankton. **[3]**

4 A student wanted to investigate the effect of different cleaning products on the growth of bacteria. She set up five agar plates that were seeded with one type of bacteria. On each plate the student placed four discs that had been soaked in a particular cleaning product. The plates were incubated at 25°C for three days. The student then measured the diameter around the discs where the bacteria hadn't grown. Her results are shown in the table below.

Plate and Cleaning Product	Diameter (mm) Around Each Disc where Bacteria Hasn't Grown				Mean (mm)
	Disc 1	Disc 2	Disc 3	Disc 4	
Plate 1 (soap)	1	2	2	1	1.5
Plate 2 (hand wash)	3	2	2	4	2.75
Plate 3 (kitchen cleaner)	5	4	6	5	5
Plate 4 (bathroom cleaner)	5	5	6	7	....
Plate 5 (no cleaner)	0	0	0	0	0

a) Complete the table by calculating the mean diameter where bacteria didn't grow for Plate 4. **[1]**

b) Which was the most effective product at killing the bacteria? **[1]**

c) Why did the student use 'Plate 5 (no cleaner)'? **[1]**

d) How has the student made her results reliable? **[1]**

HT **5** In the ocean depths, many organisms rely on marine snow. What is marine snow? **[1]**

6 Describe the process of DNA finger printing. **[6]**

✏ *The quality of written communication will be assessed in your answer to this question.*

Answers

B1 Understanding Organisms

Quick Test Answers

Page 7
1. Being overweight, stress, high alcohol intake, smoking, exercise, diet, particularly salt.
2. Mass (kg) ÷ height (m)^2
3. Arthritis, heart disease, type II diabetes, breast cancer.
4. Overpopulation, limited investment in agricultural techniques.

Page 11
1. Bacteria, fungi, viruses.
2. Harmless dead or weakened pathogen is given in an injection, the body makes antibodies which remain in the blood to fight future infection.
3. Mosquito nets, insecticides, insect repellents.

Page 14
1. **Any one from:** Knee jerk; Pupil reflex; Dropping a hot plate
2. Binocular **3.** Convex lens

Page 16
1. **Any two from:** Impaired judgement; Poor balance; Blurred vision; Slurred speech; Drowsiness; Vasodilation.
2. Red because the smoke is acidic.
3. Tar and particulates.

Page 18
1. Maintaining a constant internal environment.
2. Failure of the pancreas to produce insulin.
3. In the blood.
4. Slower

Page 21
1. Plant hormones **2.** XX **3.** Faulty genes

Answers to Exam Practice Questions
1. Lack of balance / muscle control; Blurred vision; Lack of inhibitions; Slurred speech; Drowsiness; Poor judgement; Vasodilation **[Any four for 4]**
2. a) Using a (clinical) thermometer in mouth/under armpit/in ear/in anus; Using an electronic probe in mouth/under armpit/in ear/in anus. **[Any one for 1]**
   b) Yes he could be ill; Normal body temperature is 37°C.
   c) Mucus is made **should be ticked d)** Virus
3. a) XX **b)** Alleles
4. a) Rates of smoking (males and females) have decreased; Males have a higher percentage of smoking in all years.
   b) Male cancer rates have fallen steadily; Female cancer rates have increased.
5. a) They become addicted to / dependent on nicotine.
   b) BMI = 34.6
      Yes, he is obese because his BMI is over 30.
   c) Yes, because he is obese.
   d) i) The one with LJ3; The sample size was larger.
      ii) Both drugs help people to lose weight; ULose is more effective than LJ3; But even taking a placebo resulted in some weight loss. **[Any two for 2]**
      iii) These were the control group; To prevent bias in reporting results.
   e) **Any two from:** Drug fits / blocks the receptor site / molecule; Stops the neurotransmitter getting into receptor site / molecule; Receptor is on the membrane of next neurone.
6. No, eggs are protein; Proteins are not stored in the body.

B2 Understanding Our Environment

Quick Test Answers

Page 27
1. A position or stage that an organism occupies in a food chain.
2. Crustacean, Insect, Arachnid, Myriapod
3. Heat, respiration, excretion, egestion.
4. They don't fit easily into any group.

Page 29
1. Nitrogen, carbon.
2. 78%
3. Convert ammonia to nitrates.

Page 31
1. a) Parasites
   b) **Any suitable example, e.g.** the oxpecker bird and buffalo.
2. Intraspecific.

Page 35
1. Charles Darwin
2. If they are unable to compete, due to climate change, destruction of habitat, hunting, pollution, competition.
3. **Any suitable example, e.g.** The peppered moth – dark and pale forms; Bacteria becoming resistant to antibiotics; Rats resistant to poisons.
4. They didn't agree with the Church or the Bible.

Page 37
1. Acid rain
2. Their presence or absence helps to indicate levels of pollution.
3. The amount of greenhouse gases given off in a given time per person or by an action or event.

Page 39
1. a) An animal or plant in danger of becoming extinct as numbers are so low.
   b) Protect habitats, legal protection, education programmes, captive breeding programmes, seed banks, creating artificial breeding programmes.
2. When alive – tourism; When dead – food, oil, cosmetics.
3. Sets quotas.

Answers to Exam Practice Questions
1. a) Quotas mean enough can be left to reproduce and so maintain the species.
   b) **Any two from:** Other countries may keep fishing; People may fish illegally; Global warming; Habitat destruction; Pollution; Disease; Lack of food.
2. a) Thick fur – for insulation / to keep warm / to stop heat loss; Layer of fat – for insulation; Small ears – reduce heat loss; Large feet – spread load on snow / to stop them sinking; White fur – camouflage for hunting; Fur on paws – for insulation / grip; Large body size – small SA to V / mass ratio **[Any two for 4]**
   b) **This is a model answer, which demonstrates QWC and therefore would score the full 6 marks:** The polar bear has adapted to live in a habitat of polar ice caps, so if the habitat changes, the polar bear may not be able to survive. Polar bear numbers would decline. They would no longer be camouflaged due to there being no snow or ice. Their thick coat and blubber / fat may cause them to overheat in the warmer temperatures, and the change to their habitat may lead to a lack of breeding ground.
3. a) C; No mechanisms for movement.
   b) Monera/Prokaryotes **[1]** It is single-celled; It has no nucleus. **[Any one for 1]**
   c) Animals; It uses legs (muscles) to move.
4. a) Canis lupus
   b) Zebra and donkey; Zebra and horse; Donkey and horse **[Any one for 1]** They belong to the same genus **[1]**
5. Shape reduces water loss; Thick waxy cuticle reduces water loss; Storing water in spongy layer inside stem; Green stem allows photosynthesis without leaves; Long roots to reach water; Spines to protect from animals. **[Any four for 4]**
6. a) There isn't enough energy to pass on.
   b) 120 ÷ 2200 = 5.5% **[1 for calculation, 1 for correct answer]**

B3 Living and Growing

Quick Test Answers

Page 45
1. Mitochondria.
2. A–T and C–G

Page 50
1. glucose + oxygen ➔ carbon dioxide + water + energy
2. Lactic acid
3. Sex cells (egg and sperm).
4. Sex organs (e.g. ovaries and testes).
5. Red cells, white cells, platelets, plasma.
6. Take blood from the heart to the lungs to pick up oxygen.

Page 54
1. Selective breeding.
2. Changing a person's genes in an attempt to cure a genetic disorder.
3. The production of human insulin by genetically engineered bacteria.

Page 57
1. Twins
2. Dolly the sheep.
3. Mass production of animals with desirable characteristics; Producing lots of animals which produce a human product; Producing human embryos to supply stem cells for therapy.

Answers to Exam Practice Questions

1. a) 1 = Vena cava; 2 = Pulmonary artery; 3 = Aorta; 4 = Pulmonary vein
   b) To prevent backflow / let blood flow in the right direction.
2. a) 28
   b) 40
   c) It is a similar number. Humans have 46 chromosomes, mice have 40.

3. a)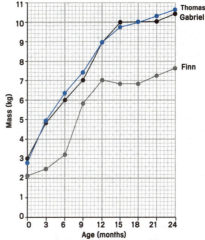
   b) Between 0 and 3 months
   c) He is healthy/No growth problems.
4. a) An identical copy of an organism.
   b) Religious or ethical suggestion, unnatural / against God / against their beliefs; Disease risk linked to transplanted organs; Money could be better spent on new medicines; Reduces variation; Possible abnormalities; Premature ageing. **[Any two for 2]**
   c) Identical twins.
   d) Nucleus removed from egg (cell) of sheep (A) **[1]** Nucleus from body cell / sheep B placed in egg (cell) **[1]** Egg (cell) implanted / put into surrogate sheep. **[1]**
   e) B because the DNA / genes / chromosomes came from sheep B.
5. a) 4
   b) T G C A

B4 It's a Green World

Quick Test Answers

Page 65
1. Pooters, sweepnets, pitfall traps, quadrats.
2. As a kite diagram.
3. Starch
4. More light, more carbon dioxide, higher temperature.

Page 69
1. Through the stomata.
2. On the underside of leaves.
3. Root cells.
4. It is the water pressure inside cells acting against the inelastic cell wall, pushing up against it. It keeps the plant upright and prevents wilting.

Page 71
1. Light, wind, temperature, humidity.
2. Cooling the plant, providing water, providing minerals, support and photosynthesis.
3. Xylem vessels are thick hollow tubes made of dead cells. Phloem is a column of living cells.

Page 74
1. Nitrates, phosphates, potassium (compounds).
2. It will have poor growth and yellow leaves.
3. Microbes, warmth, oxygen, moisture.
4. **Any six from:** Canning; Cooling; Freezing; Drying; Adding salt; Adding sugar; Pickling.

Page 77
1. Fish farming, glasshouses, hydroponics, battery farming.
2. **Any two from:** Crops are lost to pests and diseases; Organic fertilisers take time to rot and don't supply a specific balance of minerals; Expensive; More space is needed.
3. Better control of mineral levels; Better control of disease.

Answers to Exam Practice Questions

1. a) Bacteria; Fungi; Saprophyte; Decomposer **[Any one for 1]**
   b) To add more oxygen **[1]** which would allow the detritivores to respire quicker **[1]** so the matter will decompose more quickly. **[1]** If he doesn't do this, the rate of decay would decrease as there would be less oxygen for the detritivores **[1]**.
   c) Warm; Damp; Oxygen **[All three for 1]**
2. a) Xylem transports water and soluble mineral salts **[1]** from the roots to the leaves. **[1]**
   b) 1–4 **In any order:** Light; Air movement; Temperature; Humidity. **[All correct for 2]**
3. Has 6 legs; Has wings.
4. a) Quadrat
   b) Set an area; Place quadrats randomly within the area; Count the number of different plant species; Repeat several times. **[Any three for 3]**
   c) Transect
5. a) Nitrates / Nitrogen
   b) Potassium
   c) Behind library
6. a) 0
   b) Water moves from the solution into the potato by osmosis.
   c) Repeat the investigation and calculate a mean.
7. a) C **should be ticked**
   b) To allow sunlight through to the layer below.

Answers

B5 The Living Body

Quick Test Answers

Page 81
1. Ball and socket, hinge.
2. These muscles are in pairs and do opposite things. When one contracts the other relaxes.
3. Secretes synovial fluid.
4. It may cause further injury, especially to the spine.

Page 84
1. Amoeba 2. Closed
3. There are two circuits: heart to lungs and back; and heart to body and back.
4. Impulses from the SAN cause atria to contract and stimulate the AVN, impulses from the AVN cause ventricles to contract.

Page 89
1. **Any four from:** Irregular heart beat; Hole in the heart; Damaged or weak valves; Coronary heart disease; Heart attacks.
2. Haemophilia 3. Asbestosis 4. A, B, AB, O

Page 94
1. Oestrogen and progesterone
2. Produce sperm, produce testosterone
3. Carbohydrase, protease, lipase.
4. Clean the blood. Filter the blood reabsorbing water and useful substances.

Page 97
1. **Any two from:** Healthier diets/lifestyle, modern treatments, better housing, fewer industrial diseases.
2. Correct size and age, tissue match and same blood group.
3. Risk of miscarriage, decision of whether to continue with the pregnancy.

Answers to Exam Practice Questions
1. No starch molecules as they are too large; Sugar present as molecule is small; Therefore able to diffuse through partially permeable membrane.
2. a) Simple
   b) i) Hinge joint ii) Ligaments
3. a)

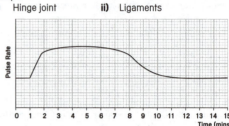

   b) To supply oxygen **[1]** and glucose **[1]** to the respiring muscles.
4. a) Oestrogen and progesterone
   b) FSH / follicle-stimulating hormone
5. a) The baby's mass increased consistently **[1]** apart from in June and September when it dipped slightly **[1]**. The baby's mass stayed within the healthy range. **[1]**
   b) 2.5kg
6. a) **Any three from:** Genes; Diet; Growth hormone; Disease; Exercise.
   b) **Any two from:** They may be family members / related; There may be a genetic link; Growth hormone problem may have been inherited
   c) Human growth hormone
7. Transfused blood possesses A antigens; John's blood has Anti-A antibodies; Antibodies will recognise A antigens as 'non-self/foreign'; A antigens are on red blood cells **[Any two for 2]** Cells carrying SA antigen will be *agglutinated*. **[1]**

B6 Beyond the Microscope

Quick Test Answers

Page 103
1. A protein coat, surrounding a strand of genetic material.
2. Spherical, rod, spiral, curved rod.
3. Through the nose (airborne microbes), mouth (contaminated food and water), skin (insect bites, cuts, needles), reproductive organs (unprotected sex).
4. Lister

Page 105
1. Making yoghurt, cheese production, vinegar production, silage production, and composting.
2. Distillation 3. Anaerobic
4. Breakdown of lactose, and production of lactic acid.

Page 107
1. **Any two from:** Alcohol, biogas, wood.
2. In a digester.
3. Alternative to fossil fuels, no net increase in greenhouse gases, no particulates produced.
4. Gasohol.

Page 110
1. Mineral particles, dead material, living organisms, air, water.
2. Provides minerals, source of water and anchorage.
3. Slugs, snails, wireworms.
4. By draining it and aerating it.

Page 113
1. Microscopic plants.
2. Oil, Sewage, PCBs, fertilisers, pesticides and detergents.
3. Fertiliser run-off into water system.
4. Organisms at the top of food chains like whales. This is because they get a huge dose of the chemical as they are at the top of the food chain.

Page 117
1. In gel beads; On reagent sticks.
2. Inserting genes from one organism into another to alter the genetic code.

3. Because the enzymes are denatured by the high temperatures. Their shape is changed so the 'key' no longer fits the 'lock'.

Answers to Exam Practice Questions
1. a) It is easier to separate the enzyme from the milk; No need to separate the enzyme and milk; Milk not contaminated; Enzyme protected in bead; It can be reused. **[Any one for 1]**
   b) To measure the glucose level in their blood.
2. **Any one from:** Enzymes are not destroyed; Enzymes work at low concentrations / only tiny amounts are needed.
   b) No, the temperature was too high / Heat destroys / denatures enzymes.
   c) i) Egg
      ii) There is protease in the washing powder; Egg is a protein; Protease breaks down egg.
3. a) Penguin, cod, squid **[All three named for 1]**
   b) i) Microscopic plants.
      ii) Temperature; Light; Availability of minerals **[All three named for 3]**
4. a) $\frac{5 + 5 + 6 + 7}{4} = \frac{23}{4} = 5.75mm$
   b) Plate 4 (bathroom cleaner)
   c) As a control that the student could compare her results against.
   d) By repeating her investigation four times.
5. The continuous shower of organic detritus falling from the upper layers of the ocean.
6. **This is a model answer, which demonstrates QWC and therefore would score the full 6 marks:** DNA fingerprinting has four main stages. A sample of DNA must first be obtained; DNA can be extracted from hair follicles, blood or semen. The DNA is then cut into fragments using restriction enzymes. A technique called electrophoresis separates the DNA fragments so that the sample can be analysed by comparing it with a reference sample, e.g. blood found at a crime scene. The analysis will show whether the DNA matches the reference sample.

Glossary of Key Words

Adaptation – the gradual change of a particular organism over generations to become better suited to its environment.

Addiction – being abnormally dependent on something; habit forming.

Aerobic respiration – respiration using oxygen, which releases energy and produces carbon dioxide and water.

Alcohol – waste product made by yeast, following anaerobic respiration.

Allele – one of two alternative forms of a particular gene.

Alveoli – tiny air sacs in the lungs where gas exchange occurs.

Amino acids – building blocks of proteins.

Anaerobic respiration – releasing energy from glucose in living cells in the absence of oxygen to produce a small amount of energy very quickly.

Antagonistic muscles – a pair of muscles that work together to create movement: when one contracts the other relaxes.

Antibiotics – medication used to kill bacterial pathogens inside the body.

Antibody – produced by white blood cells to destroy disease-causing microorganisms.

Anticoagulant – drugs used to prevent blood clotting.

Antiseptic – a chemical that kills microorganisms, but is safe to use on skin.

Artery – large blood vessel with narrow lumen and thick elastic walls (carries blood away from the lungs).

Arthropod – an invertebrate animal with an exoskeleton and segmented body and jointed legs.

Asbestosis – a lung disease caused by inhaling asbestos particles.

Aseptic – sterile conditions which prevent contamination.

Asexual – reproduction with no parent; offspring are clones.

Asthma – an illness that stops people breathing properly due to a narrowing of the airways.

Auxin – a plant hormone that affects growth and development.

Bacteria – microscopic, single-celled organism with no nucleus.

Binocular – binocular vision uses two eyes to judge distances.

Biodiversity – the variety of living organisms in an ecosystem.

Biofuel – a fuel produced by a living organism.

Biogas – fuel produced from the anaerobic decomposition of organic waste.

Biomass – the mass of matter in a living organism.

Blood pressure – the pressure of the blood in arteries and veins.

Bronchi – the branches of the trachea (windpipe).

Bronchioles – the small branches of the bronchi.

Budding – reproducing asexually by 'budding' off the parent.

Capillary – a blood vessel that connects arteries to veins; where the exchange of materials takes place.

Captivity – being held or confined to a certain space, e.g. cage.

Carbohydrates – foods that provide energy.

Carcinogens – cancer-causing chemicals.

Cardiovascular efficiency – a measure of how well your heart copes with cardiovascular exercise.

Carnivore – an animal that hunts and eats other animals.

Cartilage – smooth, connecting tissue that covers the ends of bones in a joint.

Catalyst – a substance used to speed up a chemical reaction without being chemically altered itself.

Characteristics – distinguishing features.

Chitin – material that is used in exoskeletons.

Chlorophyll – the green pigment found in most plants; responsible for photosynthesis.

Cholesterol – a type of fat that builds up in the arteries.

Chromosome – a coil of DNA made up of genes, found in the nucleus of plants/animal cells.

Circulatory system – a system of tubes and a pump to move fluids around a body. In humans, this consists of the heart and blood vessels.

Clone – a genetically identical offspring of an organism.

Clot – a mass or lump of coagulated blood.

Competition – rivalry/struggle amongst organisms for food, space, mates, etc.

Consumer – an organism that eats other organisms.

Cytoplasm – the jelly-like substance found in living cells where chemical reactions take place.

Data – information collected from an experiment/investigation.

Decay – rotting, breaking down.

Decomposers – organisms that break down dead plants or animals into simpler substances.

Deficiency – a lack of a substance.

Denature – to irreversibly change the structure of a protein molecule.

Deoxygenated – blood with no or little oxygen.

Depressants – drugs that slow the way the body works, e.g. alcohol.

Detritivore – an organism that feeds on dead organisms and the waste of living organisms.

Detritus – waste material formed from dead and decomposing plants and animals.

Diabetes – a disease caused by the failure to control blood sugar levels due to the inability of the pancreas to secrete insulin.

Differentiation – a process by which simple cells become specialised to perform a specific function.

Diffusion – the net movement of particles from an area of high concentration to an area of low concentration.

Glossary of Key Words

Digestion – the process of breaking down food into smaller soluble particles that can pass through the gut wall and into the blood.

Diploid – a full chromosome set (i.e. 46), as found in most cells of the body.

Distillation – a process used to separate liquids by evaporation followed by condensation to produce a pure liquid.

DNA (deoxyribonucleic acid) – the nucleic acid molecules that make up chromosomes in cells and carry genetic information.

Double helix – structure of DNA; twisted ladder structure.

Echocardiogram – a medical test which uses sound waves that echo against structures in the heart to build up a detailed picture of the heart.

Ecosystem – refers to a physical environment – the conditions there and the organisms that live there.

Egestion – the removal of undigested food and waste from an animal's body.

Electrocardiogram – a tracing of the electric currents that initiate the heart beat; used to diagnose heart conditions.

Embryo – an organism in the early stages of development in the uterus.

Emphysema – chronic irreversible lung disease, caused by smoking.

Endangered – organisms whose numbers are so low they are in danger of becoming extinct.

Enzyme – a protein molecule and biological catalyst found in living organisms that helps chemical reactions to take place.

Evaporation – when particles gain enough energy to leave the liquid and become a gas.

Evolve – to develop and change naturally over a period of time.

Excretion – the removal of waste products from the body.

Expiration – exhaling (breathing out) air.

Extinct – an organism that no longer exists.

Fats – a wide group of compounds that provide the body with energy and insulation, e.g. butter, oil.

Fermentation – the process by which microorganisms obtain energy and produce other substances through respiration; the process by which yeast converts sugars to alcohol and carbon dioxide through anaerobic respiration.

Fermenter – a controlled environment that maintains ideal conditions for microorganisms to carry out fermentation.

Fertilisation – the fusion of a male gamete with a female gamete.

Fertiliser – any substance used to make soil more fertile.

Flagellum – a 'whip-like' tail found on bacterial cells and used for movement.

Fossil fuels – coal, oil and gas.

FSH – (follicle-stimulating hormone) – hormone involved in the menstrual cycle.

Fungi – single-celled microscopic organisms.

Gamete – a specialised sex cell (egg and sperm).

Gene – a small section of DNA, in a chromosome, that determines a particular characteristic on its own or in combination with other genes.

Genetic engineering/modification – the alteration of the genetic make-up of an organism, e.g. by introducing new genes from another organism.

Global warming – the gradual increase in the Earth's average temperature.

Glucose – a type of sugar; plants make this during photosynthesis.

Greenhouse effect – the process by which the Earth is kept warm by the atmosphere reflecting heat back down towards the Earth, preventing it from escaping into space.

Growth – an increase in mass, length or size.

Haemoglobin – the pigment that carries oxygen in the red blood cells.

Haploid – a cell that contains just one copy of each chromosome (i.e. 23 chromosomes).

Herbivore – animals that eat plants.

Homeostasis – the maintenance of constant internal conditions in the body.

Hormone – a chemical messenger that travels around the body in the blood to affect target organs.

Host – an organism that another organism lives off.

Humus – decayed remains of animals and plants which were in the soil.

Hydroponics – a method of growing plants in a solution instead of soil or compost.

Hypothesis – a scientific explanation that will be tested through experiments.

Immunisation – giving an injection to provide immunity from a disease.

Indicator species – a species that acts as an indicator of pollution.

Inherit – to 'receive' genes or characteristics from a parent.

Insoluble – when a solid doesn't dissolve.

Inspiration – inhaling (breathing in) air.

Insulin – a hormone, produced by the pancreas, which controls blood glucose concentrations.

Intensive farming – farming which uses fertilisers and labour-saving technologies including pesticides and machinery.

Invertebrate – an animal with no backbone.

***In vitro* fertilisation (IVF)** – fertilisation that takes place outside the body, usually in a Petri dish.

Kwashiorkor – an illness caused by protein deficiency due to lack of food.

Lactic acid – a waste product from anaerobic respiration in animals.

LH – (luteinising hormone) – involved in the menstrual cycle, works with FSH.

Ligament – the tissue that connects a bone to a joint.

Menstrual cycle – the monthly shedding of the uterus lining and unfertilised egg.

Meristem – an area where unspecialised cells divide, producing plant growth, e.g. roots, shoots.

Microorganism – an organism that can only be seen with a microscope, e.g. bacteria.

Meiosis – cell division in reproductive tissue, which produces gametes with a half-chromosome set.

Mitochondria – the structures in the cytoplasm of a cell where energy is produced through respiration reactions.

Mitosis – the type of cell division that forms two daughter cells, each with the same number of chromosomes as the parent cell.

Model – a representation of a system or idea, used to describe or explain the system or idea.

Monocular – each eye is used separately to increase the field of view.

Mutation – a spontaneous change in the genetic material of a cell.

Mutualism – a relationship that benefits both organisms.

Natural selection – the process by which organisms that are better adapted to their environment are able to survive and reproduce.

Neurone – a specialised cell that transmits electrical messages (nerve impulses) when stimulated.

Nitrates – compounds containing nitrogen; plants need nitrates for growth.

Nucleus – the control centre of a cell.

Nutrients – substances used in an organism's metabolism which must be taken in from its environment.

Organic farming – involves farming without the use of chemicals, artificial fertilisers, pesticides or herbicides.

Osmosis – the net movement of water particles from a dilute solution to a more concentrated solution across a partially permeable membrane.

Ovary – the female reproductive organ that produces eggs.

Oxygenated – with/containing oxygen.

Ozone – a gas in the Earth's atmosphere.

Pacemaker – the group of cells that control the beating of the heart.

Parasite – an organism that lives off another organism.

Pasteurisation – the heat treatment of liquids which prolong their shelf life by limiting bacterial growth.

Pathogen – a disease-causing microorganism.

Penicillin – an antibiotic/chemical that kills bacteria; used to treat infections.

Pest – an organism that causes damage or harm.

Pesticide – a chemical that kills pests.

Photosynthesis – the chemical process that takes place in green plants where water combines with carbon dioxide to produce glucose using light energy.

Plankton – microscopic plants (phytoplankton) and animals (zooplankton) that float in water.

Pollution – the contamination of an environment by chemicals, waste or heat.

Pooter – apparatus used to collect insects.

Population – a group of organisms of the same species living in a defined area.

Predator – an animal that hunts, kills and eats its prey.

Prey – an animal that is hunted, killed and eaten by a predator.

Producers – organisms that produce biomass when they photosynthesise, i.e. green plants; organisms that occupy the first trophic level of a food chain.

Proteins – large organic compounds made of amino acids; needed in the diet for growth and repair.

Protista – kingdom made of unicellular organisms.

Protozoa – single-celled microscopic animals.

Pyramid of biomass – shows the energy flow through an ecosystem; always pyramid shaped.

Pyramid of numbers – shows how many organisms are at each stage of a food chain; not always pyramid shaped.

Quadrat – a square of known size used in ecology to sample an area randomly.

Receptor – the part of the nervous system that detects a stimulus; a sense organ, e.g. eyes, ears.

Recovery rate – the time it takes for your heart rate to return to normal after exercise.

Reflex action – an involuntary action; a fast, involuntary response to a stimulus.

Residual air – the amount of gas remaining in the lung at the end of a maximal exhalation.

Respiration – a process that takes place in cells, which releases energy from glucose.

Respiratory system – where gas exchange occurs, e.g. the lungs in humans or gills in fish.

Retina – the back of the eye; contains light sensitive cells/receptors.

Selective breeding – the process by which animals are selected and mated to produce offspring with desirable characteristics.

Skeleton – the supporting framework of an animal's body.

Soluble – when a substance dissolves.

Specialisation – the development or adaptation of a particular body part for a specific function.

Glossary of Key Words

Species – smallest group/type of organisms; second part of binomial name. A species of organisms have similar characteristics.

Stem cells – cells from human embryos or adult bone marrow that have yet to differentiate.

Stimulants – chemicals that speed up the heart and nervous system, e.g. caffeine.

Stomata – the tiny openings on a plant leaf used for gas exchange.

Surrogacy – carrying and delivering a baby to give to someone else. Usually the baby is not genetically linked to the surrogate.

Sustainable – to maintain and keep in existence.

Sweepnet – a large net used to catch insects so they can be counted or studied.

Synovial joint – type of joint allowing movement in places such as elbow and knee.

Tidal air – the volume of air inhaled and exhaled at each breath.

Toxin – a poison produced by a living organism.

Trachea – the windpipe (through which air gets to the lungs).

Transect – a sampling method.

Transgenic organism – an organism that has had new genes inserted into it.

Translocation – the transportation of food through phloem in plants.

Transpiration – the loss of water (by diffusion and evaporation) from plants, especially from their leaves.

Variable – something that changes during the course of an experiment/investigation.

Variation – the differences between individuals of the same species.

Vein – a type of blood vessel that transports blood towards the heart.

Ventilation – breathing.

Virus – a tiny microorganism with a very simple structure.

Vital capacity – the volume of air that can be exhaled from the lungs after the deepest possible breath has been taken.

Yeast – a single-celled organism used to make alcohol and to make bread rise; reproduce asexually.

HT Active transport – the movement of substances against a concentration gradient; requires energy.

Agglutinin – an agglutinin is a substance that causes particles to coagulate to form a thickened mass. Agglutinins can be antibodies that cause antigens to aggregate by binding to the antigen-binding sites of antibodies.

Anti-diuretic hormone (ADH) – a hormone that controls the amount of water reabsorbed by the kidneys and, therefore, the concentration of urine.

Benign – a growth or tumour that isn't usually dangerous to health, not progressive or recurrent; does not spread all over the body.

Carbon footprint – the total set of greenhouse gases or emissions caused by an organisation, event, or person.

Contractile vacuole – a tiny organelle found in some organisms that pumps fluid in a cyclical manner from within the cell to the outside; helps maintain water balance.

Emulsify – to break down fats into small droplets to form an emulsion.

Extremophiles – microbes that thrive in physically or geochemically extreme conditions that are detrimental to most life on Earth.

Flaccid – a plant cell that isn't rigid; it is floppy due to lack of water.

Generalist – an organism that can utilise many food sources and therefore is able to flourish in many habitats.

Genotype – the genetic make-up of an individual, usually given letters to represent different genes, e.g. Bb.

Heterozygous – to have different alleles in a gene pair.

Homozygous – to have the same alleles in a gene pair.

Hybrid – the infertile offspring of two different species.

Immunosuppressive drugs – drugs which dampen down the immune system.

Limiting factor – a factor that limits the rate of reaction.

Malignant – a tumour that becomes progressively worse, and spreads around the body.

Marine snow – a continuous shower of mostly organic detritus falling from the upper layers of the ocean.

Ossification – the replacement of cartilage with sodium and phosphorus salts to make bones hard during growth.

Oxyhaemoglobin – haemoglobin combined with oxygen.

Phenotype – the outward expression of a gene, e.g. blue eyes.

Plasmolysis – the contraction of the inside of plant cells due to the loss of water.

Ribosomes – tiny organelles in the cell that carry out protein synthesis.

Saprophytes – bacteria and fungi that feed on dead organic material.

Specialist – an organism which has a small range of adaptations.

Synapse – the small gap between adjacent neurones.

Thrombosis – a blood clot.

Turgid – a rigid plant cell.

Ultrafiltration – the process that takes place in the kidneys in which water and molecules are squeezed out of the blood into the tubules.

Vasoconstriction – the narrowing of the blood vessels to reduce heat loss from the surface of the skin.

Vasodilation – the widening of the blood vessels to increase heat loss from the surface of the skin.

Zonation – distribution of organisms in an area; sampling method.